Ireland's Love Poems

W. W. Norton & Company • New York London

IRELAND'S
LOVE
POEMS

————✠————

WONDER AND A WILD DESIRE

Edited by A. Norman Jeffares

For information about permission to reproduce selections from this book, write to
Permissions, W. W. Norton & Company, Inc., 500 Fifth Avenue, New York,
NY 10110

The text of this book is composed in Centaur with display set in Centaur
Composition by Tom Ernst
Manufacturing by Courier Westford
Book Design by Blue Shoe Studio

Library of Congress Cataloging-in-Publication Data

Ireland's love poems: wonder and wild desire / edited by A. Norman Jeffares
p. cm.
Includes index.
ISBN 0-393-04316-9
1. Love poetry, English—Irish authors. 2. Love poetry, Irish—Translations into
English.
3. Ireland—Poetry. I. Title: Love poems. II. Jeffares, A. Norman
(Alexander Norman), 1920–

PR8861.L6 174 2002
821.008'03543'09417—dc21   2001044706

W. W. Norton & Company, Inc., 500 Fifth Avenue, New York, N.Y. 10110
www.wwnorton.com

W. W. Norton & Company Ltd., Castle House, 75/76 Wells Street, London
W1T 3QT

1 2 3 4 5 6 7 8 9 0

TO THURLOE AND JACQUELINE

Contents

＊—✦—＊

Introduction

⸺ ⊨⊹⊨ ⸺

Irish love poetry reflects the traditions and attitudes of the island's various civilizations, changing with their development or decline. There is, therefore, a rich and varied inheritance of love poems in Irish and English to which poets are constantly adding, and there is a fine stock of excellent translations of Irish originals into English.

This introduction offers some suggestions of historical turning points which have affected the course of Irish love poetry. Contemporary Irish love poetry written by women is forthright, for feminism has affected many women writers in their reactions against what was a male-dominated society. But Irish women's independence seen against past history is nothing new. In the pagan period when the Brehon Laws held sway the role of women in society was not circumscribed. Their independence is reflected in the love stories of the early heroic sagas, the tales of the Ulster cycle and the Fenian. They could often take a leading role in courtship as we see, for instance, in Deirdre's approach to Naoise. On her birth Cathbad the druid had prophesied that she would bring untold ruin upon Ulster. She was being brought up in segregation as a future bride for Conchobar, King of Ulster, when she saw a raven drinking the blood of a calf slaughtered in the snow. She thought of a husband with black hair, red cheeks and white skin. Naoise, one of the King's warriors, fitted this desirable imagery. When he was alone outside, she went out and made as if to pass him by. Not recognising her, he remarked

> 'Beautiful is the heifer going by me.'
> 'Heifers' said she, 'are bound to be big when there are no bulls.'
> 'The bull of the province is with you,' he said, 'namely the King of the Ulstermen.'
> 'I would choose between the two of you', she said, 'and I would take a young bull like you.'
> 'By no means!' said he, 'even because of Cathbad's prophecy.'
> 'Do you say that in order to reject me?'
> 'It will indeed be for that reason', he said.
> With that she made a leap at him and seized the two ears on his head.
> 'Two ears of shame and division are these', said she, 'unless you take me away with you.'

So Naoise took her off to Scotland, accompanied by his brothers, with disastrous consequences for all concerned; when they returned to Ireland, Naoise and his brothers were treacherously murdered by the jealous and revenge-seeking Conchobar. Deirdre maintained her freedom to the end, committing suicide when Conchobar claimed her.

The Fenian cycle has a similar story of the sexual overtures of Grainne, daughter of Cormac the High King of Tara. She had agreed to marry Fin mac Cumhaill, the elderly leader of the Fianna: however, she gives a sleeping draught to those people most likely to hinder her plans, and, Finn's son Oisin having refused her, she places Diarmuid O'Duibhne under *geas* (a form of taboo) to run off with her. At first, out of loyalty to Finn, he does not sleep with her, but does so later as a result of her taunting him. Like Deirdre, Grainne has made the running. A peace between Finn and the runaway lovers is arranged: they live in Sligo and have four sons, but Diarmuid dies, wounded by a boar, not given healing water by Finn who lets it run through his fingers. Like Deirdre's love affair it ends in tragedy.

The Gaelic Brehon Laws, the texts of which date from about the seventh or eighth centuries AD, show us an Irish society in which women could divorce husbands for, *inter alia*, impotence, imbecility, physical assault or failure to maintain them. The status of women with professional qualifications (in, say, medicine or crafts) was recognised, and women without brothers who inherited could administer holdings. There were several categories of marriage, secondary wives being recognised as well as a principal wife, and ten categories of marriage regulated the husband's position. We can see something of such marriage arrangements in the *Tain Bo Cuailnge* in *The Book of Leinster*, where Maeve addresses her husband Ailill and spells out why she chose him. He was neither mean nor timid nor jealous and so could match her in generosity and bravery, while it would not have done for him to be jealous, for, she said, she was 'never without a man in the shadow by her'.

It is possible to find various symbolic markers in Irish history which indicate changes in society. The Brehon Code was probably fully developed when St Patrick's arrival in Ireland in 432 brought Christianity to the island and the power of the druids was diminished as a result. Christian monasteries had increased in number by the seventh century. The study of Latin flourished in them and Irish writing was adapted to the Latin alphabet. The monks created magnificent illuminated manuscript books, such as the eighth or ninth century *Book of Kells* (a Latin copy of the four Gospels) or the twelfth century *Book of Leinster*, its medieval Irish learning including the *Tain Bo Cuailnge*, the epic tale of the Ulster cycle, and *The Lebor Gabala Erenn*, a legendary history of Ireland from the creation to the twelfth century. It was through the monasteries that much of the earlier pagan literature was preserved.

After the Norman invasion of 1170 the Normans became 'more Irish than the Irish themselves', marrying into Irish families, Gaelicizing their homes and adopting many Irish ways of life. As well as bringing their feudal system of government into Ireland they also introduced *amour courtois* into Ireland's aristocratic society, following the example of that society by becoming patrons of the native Irish poets. The poets had preserved their powerful pre-Christian status: from the twelfth to the seventeenth century the *fili* and bards were highly respected members of society. They were thoroughly trained over a long period in bardic schools. Parallel and complementary to the monastic centres of learning, these schools were often attached to poetic families, for the poets became in effect an hereditary caste, responsible in part for preserving traditional knowledge. They had developed a formal literary language and style and now applied their sophisticated literary wit to the *danta gradha*, love poems. These were also written by some members of aristocratic families, Gerald Fitzgerald, the fourth Earl of Desmond (1333–1398), being the first known poet of Norman origin to have written courtly love poems in Irish.

English attitudes to Irish bards were stern. In 1366 the Statutes of Kilkenny had forbidden English settlers in Ireland to maintain or entertain Irish minstrels, poets or storytellers, a prohibition renewed in 1536. Elizabethan attitudes were more severe. O'Brien, Earl of Thomond, was forced to hang three distinguished Irish poets. The reasons for this persecution of the poets is made clear in the English poet Edmund Spenser's *View of the Present State of Ireland* (1596). While revealing his appreciation of the 'sweet wit and good invention' of the Irish poets (whose work he had translated for him) their writings seeming 'sprinkled with some pretty flowers of their own natural device which gave good grace and comeliness into them', he nonetheless thought their poems graced wickedness and vice. The trouble was that the Irish bards kept alive the traditions and identity of an aristocratic Irish civilisation and had a dangerous desire 'to maintain their own lewd liberty'.

The clash of the two cultures came to a turning point with the Flight of the Earls in 1607, when Hugh of Tyrconnel left Ireland for Rome. This was the result of harassment from the English (and from Irish rivals) after the Battle of Kinsale (1601) in which the Earl's forces and a 4,000 strong Spanish expedition to Ireland were defeated. The Flight signified the virtual end of the Irish aristocracy and, though many distinguished Irish poets were writing in the seventeenth century, the bardic order collapsed with the loss of its patrons and the security for which they had stood.

Poetry changed, and love poetry particularly: song metres replaced the complex classical bardic forms as the old Gaelic society disintegrated and scattered schools of poetry were able to maintain only vestiges of the tradition. Love poetry became simpler, more spontaneous. It was joined by the *Aisling*, in which a female persona represents Ireland and prophesies the return of a Stuart king; it was a blend of political and amatory poetry, the genre going back to the seventh century, though it now flourished afresh in the seventeenth and, especially, the eighteenth centuries.

Writing in English from the medieval period has not survived in any quantity, though a theme that recurs through Irish love poetry appeared in a lyric recorded in the Red Book of Ossory, collected by Richard Ledrede, the bishop of Ossory (1316–1360), a lament of a young girl married to an old man:

Alas how should I sing?
Yloren is my playing.
How should I with that old man
To leven and leave my leman,
Sweetest of all thing?

The fourteenth century poem 'Icham of Irlaunde' is better known, well translated by W. B. Yeats as 'I am of Ireland', with its invitation to 'come ant daunce wyt me/In Irlaunde.' Another fourteenth century love poem is simpler:

Lou, lou lou! Wer he goth!
A lou, lou lou wer he goth!
For hir les myn haly water-ter-ter
Lov! [lou].

There are some examples of popular writing in English by the seventeenth century but these do not have any particularly Irish qualities. These emerged more clearly in the eighteenth century, but shaped by neoclassicism. Many of the writers in English had been educated in Greek and Latin at Trinity College, Dublin, and those of them who became playwrights naturally included some love poems in the form of songs in their dramas. The tone was set by Nahum Tate's fashionable Ardelias, Daphnes and Julias with their swains mournfully vocal in shady groves, a line continued elegantly by Thomas Parnell, while William Congreve, George Farquhar and Richard Steele—to mention but a few among the many Irish dramatists who appealed to London audiences—also embodied lyrics very successfully in their dramas: their example was followed by Goldsmith and Sheridan. Swift, however, had earlier let his wit loose on mock-pastorals and written decidedly anti-romantic views of brides in the realities of the bedroom.

Yet again historical events mark changes in Irish writing. The rebellion of 1798 was followed by the Act of Union of 1800 which removed Dublin's status as a seat of government and, in effect, brought an end to the years of Anglo-Irish achievement, so well exemplified in art and neoclassical and Palladian architecture and in plaster work, furniture, silver, glass and cutlery. Romantic literature had begun to oust neoclassicism, and in Ireland it was bound up with a rediscovery of Irish literature and tradition.

Joseph Cooper Walker's *Historical Memoirs of the Irish Bards* (1786) was followed by Charlotte Brooke's influential *Reliques of Irish Poetry* (1789). There was a new interest in Irish music, exemplified by Edward Bunting's publication of three *Collections* of the ancient music of Ireland. At first this turning to the Irish past, to music, poetry and legends, was largely antiquarian. Soon, however, it blended with patriotism in Thomas Moore's plangent, emotive songs as it did in the novels of Lady Morgan and Charles Robert Maturin. Minor poets such as George Darley and Aubrey De Vere wrote effective love poetry, aware of their Irish inheritance, as did the novelist Gerald Griffin, Jeremiah J. Callanan, the translator and collector of folk lore and poetry who aimed to match Thomas Moore with a collection of Munster melodies, and, perhaps surprisingly, the novelist, painter and song writer Samuel Lover.

The poetic achievement became more impressive with the highly individual approach of James Clarence Mangan, expert at capturing the assonance, the flowing, singing notes of Irish poetry. As well as some of his intensely romantic poems such as 'And Then No More' and 'The Lover's Farewell' he is chiefly known for his 'Dark Rosaleen', written within the *Aisling* convention. Mangan was one of a group of scholars and researchers who worked for the Irish Ordnance survey under the direction of Sir George Petrie: they produced many poems and translations as well as scholarly works such as Eugene O'Curry's *Lectures and Manuscript Materials of Ancient Irish History* (1861) and *Manners and Customs of the Ancient Irish* (1873).

It was, however, Sir Samuel Ferguson whose vigorous translations brought Irish poetry, and particularly Irish love poetry, to a wider public's attention. He wanted to play his part in 'the formation of a characteristic school of letters' in his own country. He contributed articles and translations to various journals from 1832 on. His *Lays of the Western Gael* appeared in 1865, his *Congal* in 1872, and his *Poems* (1880) collected his shorter pieces. Alongside his vivid translations with their impressive narrative energy, appeared the prose works of Standish James O'Grady, whose *History of Ireland: the Heroic Period* (1878) and *Early Bardic Literature, Ireland* (1879) were followed by a *History of Ireland: Cuchulain and his Contemporaries* (1880) and *Cuchulain: an Epic* (1882). O'Grady attempted to convey the grandeur and nobility of the Ulster Cycle and the Fenian Cycle, and had a most stimulating effect on younger writers.

Yet another historical event and its effects must be, however, considered here, the great mid-century famine, which began in 1845 and lasted until 1849. This calamitous failure of the potato crop from blight was a watershed in Ireland's nineteenth century history. Before it the population, half of it Irish-speaking, amounted to about eight million people. They married young; they were lively, uninhibited, given to dancing and drinking, but very many of them lived at subsistence level, depending upon the potato, cultivating small sub-divided plots of land. Ireland was very poor, and as a result of the famine—with its ensuing starvation leading to typhus, with its evictions and with its emigration on a vast scale—the country's eight million people had become six and a half million by the census of 1851: about a million died and half a million emigrated. (By 1911 the population was four million, four hundred thousand.) The effect of this disaster was profound. A new puritanism combined with the Temperance Movement led by Father Mathew (1790–1856) to change Irish attitudes: life lived exuberantly and often violently before the Famine now became very precious.

As the country slowly recovered, politics became paramount. Political extremism led to the Fenian movement which started among Irish-Americans, its members bound by oath to secrecy, their aim the removal of English control of Ireland and the establishment of an independent Irish republic. After the failure of their rising in Ireland in 1867 they supported the Land League, founded in 1879. During the Land Wars of the eighteen eighties, Charles Stewart Parnell, himself a landlord, provided political leadership within—and without—Westminster. Ireland was eventually transformed through the Ashbourne Act of 1885 and the Wyndham Act of 1903 which, building on Gladstone's earlier measures, bought out the landlords and effectively turned Ireland into a land of peasant proprietors (they were later categorised as 'twenty acre capitalists').

The political turmoil of the eighteen eighties subsided into ineffectual bitterness when Parnell's involvement in a divorce case led to his repudiation by the English Liberal Party and the consequent split in the Irish party between those who supported and those who rejected him as leader. With Parnell's death in 1891 W. B. Yeats thought the time opportune to launch the Irish literary movement. Though Yeats was a convinced nationalist, his love poetry was escapist, dreamy, beautiful and idealist. He wanted to make a new literature for Ireland by drawing on past Irish legend and literature, locating poetry in Irish settings, but avoiding the rhetoric and clichés which had marked Irish patriotic poetry in the nineteenth century.

Just as he had been influenced by Ferguson and O'Grady so he influenced many poets who imitated his dreamy, symbolic Celtic twilight love poetry. But he began to change his delicate, adjectival, romantic style at the turn of the century, stripping off the pre-Raphaelite decoration and introducing an increasing note of realism into his poetry. He was to be equally influential in his new way of writing, which first celebrated his past love for Maud Gonne (she had married John MacBride in 1903) and then moved on to the contemplation of human love and passion—and the frustrations of old age!—in his great, powerful poems of the nineteen twenties and thirties, often metaphysical, precise now in their symbolism. While the change was apparent earlier, his own very direct poem 'Easter 1916' marks the effect of the martyrdom of the Irish leaders shot for their part in the Easter Rising, the beginning of the savage struggle which led to the establishment of the Irish Free State in 1922 and the subsequent vicious civil war between de Valera's extreme republicans and those who supported the Treaty.

The new Free State proved censorious: literature was regarded with suspicion, and much frustration ensued for Irish writers as the notorious Censorship Board took its toll of their writing. Gradually, however, after the de Valera epoch poets and novelists felt freer to speak out. Austin Clarke, for instance, had a poetic rebirth and began—he who had started to write in the 'Celtic twilight' style—to pack his poems with eroticism and sensuality in the nineteen sixties and seventies. Now women poets exercise a freedom of expression undreamed of before the sixties. The wheel has perhaps turned its circle back to that earlier Irish society when women could be outspoken queens and warriors and could pick their men in a matrilineal society.

And what of Irish men today? How will their love poetry turn out in a society of changing roles as described by Jeremy Young in his poem 'The New Man':

It used to be enough to be a knight
Who never washed or pressed a shirt of mail,
And never raised a little fingernail
To make a meal or set a house aright.

It used to be enough to joust and fight
And go upon the Quest to find the Grail;
Such manly escapades would never fail
To win the maid whose charms were his delight.

It used to be enough . . . but new men now
Must dress their kids and take them off to school,
Then battle with a supermarket queue,

And cook and clean to please their mates somehow;
For modern women count that girl a fool
Who does the work which women used to do.

ACKNOWLEDGEMENTS

Several friends have been most helpful in assisting me to discover some hitherto unpublished texts and to track down some obscure dates. I should like to express my appreciation of their kindness here. They are Professor Warwick Gould, Professor Brendan Kennelly, Professor Colin Smythe, Dr Bruce Stewart, Dr Loreto Todd, Ms Deirdre Toomey, Dr Peter van de Kamp and Professor Robert Welch.

IRELAND'S LOVE POEMS

MÁIRE MHAC AN TSAOI

Jack

From her own Irish poem

A fair-haired strapping fellow, six foot tall,
A farmer's son from Western parts,
Who won't remember how that I one night,
On a cement floor, stood with him to dance . . .

But I will not forget his arms around me,
His quiet laughter nor his civil talk—
Wearing his white shirt, and his new-combed hair
Yellow under the lamplight, scant of oil . . .

His father in his will, will leave him land,
He will take wife and he will rear his seed,
But none will ever see him as I saw him,
To none beholden, since my heart so prized him.

May he forever prosper in that measure!
May luck and joy attend him where he goes!
May his achievement level with his promise!
He was my chosen partner this summer.

ELEANOR HULL

What Is Love?

From the Irish of The Wooing of Etain

A love much-enduring through a year is my love,
It is grief close-hidden,
It is stretching, of strength beyond its bounds,
It is all the four quarters of the world;
It is the highest height of heaven;
It is breaking of the neck,
It is battle with a spectre,
It is drowning with water,
It is a race against heaven,
It is champion-feats beneath the sea,
It is wooing the echo;
So is my love, and my passion, and my devotion to her to whom I gave
   them.

John O'Keefe

Amo, Amas, I Love a Lass

Amo, Amas
I love a lass
As a cedar tall and slender!
Sweet cowslips' grace
Is her Nominative Case,
And she's of the Feminine Gender.

Rorum, corum, sunt Divorum!
Harum scarum Divo!
Tag rag, merry derry, periwig and hatband,
Hic, hac, horum Genetivo!

Can I decline
A Nymph divine?
Her voice as a flute is *dulcis*!
Her *oculi* bright!
Her *manus* white!
And soft, when I *tacto*, her pulse is!

Rorum, corum, sunt divorum!
Harum scarum Divo!
Tag rag, merry derry, periwig and hatband,
Hic, hac, horum Genetivo!

O, how bella
Is my Puella!
I'll kiss s[ae]culorum!
If I've luck, Sir!
She's my Uxor!
O, dies benedictorum!

Rorum, corum, sunt divorum!
Harum scarum Divò!
Tag rag, merry derry, periwig and hatband,
Hic, hac, horum Genetivo!

Jonathan Swift

A Pastoral Dialogue

A nymph and swain, Sheelah and Dermot hight,
Who wont to weed the court of Gosford knight,
While each with stubbed knife removed the roots
That raised between the stones their daily shoots;
As at their work they sat in counterview,
With mutual beauty smit, their passion grew.
Sing, heavenly muse, in sweetly flowing strain,
The soft endearments of the nymph and swain.

Dermot
My love to Sheelah is more firmly fixed
Than strongest weeds that grow these stones betwixt:
My spud these nettles from the stones can part,
No knife so keen to weed thee from my heart.

Sheelah
My love for gentle Dermot faster grows
Than yon tall dock that rises to thy nose.
Cut down the dock, 'twill sprout again: but O!
Love rooted out, again will never grow.

Dermot
No more that briar thy tender leg shall rake:

(I spare the thistle for Sir Arthur's sake.)
Sharp are the stones, take thou this rushy mat;
The hardest bum will bruise with sitting squat.

Sheelah
Thy breeches torn behind, stand gaping wide;
This petticoat shall save thy dear backside;
Nor need I blush, although you feel it wet;
Dermot, I vow, 'tis nothing else but sweat.

Dermot
At an old stubborn root I chanced to tug,
When the Dean threw me this tobacco plug:
A longer ha'porth never did I see;
This, dearest Sheelah, thou shalt share with me.

Sheelah
In at the pantry door this morn I slipped,
And from the shelf a charming crust I whipped:
Dennis was out, and I got hither safe;
And thou, my dear, shalt have the bigger half.

Dermot
When you saw Tady at long-bullets play,
You sat and loused him all the sunshine day.
How could you, Sheelah, listen to his tales,
Or crack such lice as his betwixt your nails?

Sheelah

When you with Oonagh stood behind a ditch,
I peeped, and saw you kiss the dirty bitch.
Dermot, how could you touch those nasty sluts!
I almost wish this spud were in your guts.

Dermot

If Oonagh once I kissed, forbear to chide:
Her aunt's my gossip by my father's side:
But, if I ever touch her lips again,
May I be doomed for life to weed in rain.

Sheelah

Dermot, I swear, though Tady's locks could hold
Ten thousand lice, and every louse was gold,
Him on my lap you never more should see;
Or may I lose my weeding-knife—and thee.

Dermot

O, could I earn for thee, my lovely lass,
A pair of brogues to bear thee dry to mass!
But see where Norah with the sowens comes—
Then let us rise, and rest our weary bums.

William Congreve

Song

A nymph and a swain to Apollo once prayed,
The swain had been jilted, the nymph been betrayed,
Their intent was to try if his oracle knew
E'er a nymph that was chaste, or a swain that was true.

Apollo was mute, and had like t' have been posed,
But sagely at length he this secret disclosed:
He alone won't betray in whom none will confide,
And the nymph may be chaste that has never been tried.

GERALD GRIFFIN

Song

A place in thy memory, dearest,
Is all that I claim,
To pause and look back when thou hearest
The sound of my name.
Another may woo thee nearer,
Another may win and wear;
I care not, though he be dearer,
If I am remembered there.

Could I be thy true lover, dearest,
Couldst thou smile on me,
I would be the fondest and nearest
That ever loved thee.
But a cloud o'er my pathway is glooming
Which never must break upon thine,
And Heaven, which made thee all blooming,
Ne'er made thee to wither on mine.

Remember me not as a lover
Whose fond hopes are crossed,
Whose bosom can never recover
The light it has lost;

As the young bride remembers the mother,
She loves, yet never may see,
As a sister remembers a brother,
Oh, dearest, remember me.

WILLIAM ALLINGHAM

An Evening

A sunset's moulded cloud;
A diamond evening-star;
Sad blue hills afar;
Love in his shroud.

Scarcely a tear to shed;
Hardly a word to say;
The end of a summer day;
Sweet love dead.

W. R. RODGERS

The Lovers

After the tiff there was stiff silence, till
One word flung in centre like single stone,
Starred and cracked the ice of her resentment
To its edge. From that stung core opened and
Poured up one outward and widening wave
Of eager and extravagant anger.

Denis Devlin

Wishes for Her

Against Minoan sunlight
Slight-boned head,
Buildings with the thin climb of larks
Trilling off whetstone brilliants,
Slight head, nor petal nor marble
Night-shell
Two, one and separate.

Love in loving, all
A fledging, hard-billed April,
Soil's gaudy chemistry in fission and fuse.
And she
Lit out of fire and glass
Lightning
The blue flowers of vacant thunder.

In the riverlands
Strained with old battlefields, old armor
In which their child, rust, sighs,
Strangers lost in the courtyard,
I lie awake.
The ice recedes, on black silk
Rocks the seals sway their heads.

No prophet deaths
In the webbed tensions of memory,
No harm
Night lean with hunters.
I wish you well, wish
Tall angels whose rib-freezing
Beauty attends you.

ROBIN FLOWER

At Mass

From the Irish

Ah! light lovely lady with delicate lips aglow,
With breast more white than a branch heavy-laden with snow,
When my hand was uplifted at Mass to salute the Host
I looked at you once, and the half of my soul was lost.

KATHARINE TYNAN

Blind Country

Ah love, the skies were always raining
The wind was crying through the day
Like a grieved heart that goes complaining
And finds no other thing to say
Sad-foot the sparrow went and starling,
The robin's breast was washed of red
A thrush was singing to his darling
No violet in the garden-bed.

Ah, love, but you and I together
Built bowers of blossoms in the South,
And Summer in the Wintry weather,
And songs, like honey in the mouth,—
Ah love, our Eden worth the gaining
Where never a jewelled snake might be,
In a green land of wind and raining
Between the ocean and the sea!

OLIVER GOLDSMITH

Song

Ah, me! When shall I marry me?
Lovers are plenty; but fail to relieve me.
He, fond youth, that could carry me,
Offers to love, but means to deceive me.

But I will rally, and combat the ruiner:
Not a look, not a smile shall my passion discover:
She that gives all to the false one pursuing her,
Makes but a penitent, loses a lover.

PADRAIC FALLON

The Poems of Love

All the poems of love are one;
All women too. The name that runs
Profanely between love and lover
Is the name repeated over
In the rosaries of nuns
All the poems of love are one.

Solar red, masochist black,
There's precedent for each in heaven;
Whatever be a body's leaven
The rosaries of the holy nation
Thrill to some transfiguration.
Love makes up the thing we lack.

All the women Tom or Jack
Buy or bed, the slumtown tits
Have bright otherworld habits;
A queen shares pillows with a clown,
Still nebulously wears her crown
And is most royal on her back.

When Tom and his hedge mistress come
Drunken to the judgement seat,

The obscene measures on his tongue
Start the heavens into song;
Endlessly must Tom recite
The love he made by rule of thumb.

And brawling face and bawling gums
Fade fawnlike into some young grace;
Love lives serenely many ways;
Love lives in all that it may not lack
Its body in riots, drunks and drums
And all the rosaries of nuns in black.

CHARLES J. KICKHAM

Slievenamon

Alone, all alone, by the wave-washed strand,
And alone in the crowded hall.
The hall it is gay, and the waves they are grand,
But my heart is not here at all!
It flies far away, by night and by day,
To the time and the joys that are gone!
And I never can forget the sweet maiden I met,
In the Valley near Slievenamon.

It was not the grace of her queenly air,
Nor her cheek of the rose's glow,
Nor her soft black eyes, nor her flowing hair,
Nor was it her lily-white brow.
'Twas the soul of truth and of melting ruth,
And the smile like a summer dawn,
That stole my heart away one soft summer day,
In the Valley near Slievenamon.

In the festive hall, by the star-watched shore,
Ever my restless spirit cries:
'My love, oh, my love, shall I ne'er see you more?
And, my land, will you never uprise?

By night and by day, I ever, ever, pray,
While lonely my life flows on,
To see our flag unrolled, and my true love to enfold,
In the Valley near Slievenamon.

Nuala Ní Dhomhnaill

Shannon Estuary 1988

And I will sing a lullaby
To my lover
Wave on wave,
Stave upon half-stave,
My phosphorescence as bed-linen under him;
My favourite, whom I, from afar have chosen.

OLIVER ST JOHN GOGARTY

Good Luck

Apples of gold the Hero dropt
As he was in the race outstript;
And Atalanta, running, stopt,
And all her lovely body dipt
A moment; but she lost her stride—
And had to go to bed a bride.

And was it not a cordial strong,
By which the young Iseult was filled
With passion for a whole life long;
For that the amorous juice instilled?
So he who kept the unwitting tryst
Was sure of love before he kissed.

But where can I get Western gold,
Or posset of constraining fire?—
I who am fated to behold
Beauty outdistancing desire?
Aye, and to falter wonder-struck;
There's no good love without good luck!

EDWARD LYSAGHT

Kitty of Coleraine

As beautiful Kitty one morning was tripping
With a pitcher of milk, from the fair of Coleraine,
When she saw me she stumbled, the pitcher it tumbled,
And all the sweet buttermilk watered the plain.

'O, what shall I do now?—'twas looking at you now!
Sure, sure such a pitcher I'll ne'er meet again!
'Twas the pride of my dairy: O Barney M'Cleary!
You're sent as a plague to the girls of Coleraine.'

I sat down beside her, and gently did chide her,
That such a misfortune should give her such pain.
A kiss then I gave her; and ere did I leave her,
She vowed for such pleasure she'd break it again.

'Twas hay-making season—I can't tell the reason—
Misfortunes will never come single, 'tis plain;
For very soon after poor Kitty's disaster
The devil a pitcher was whole in Coleraine

KATHARINE TYNAN

The Dead-Tryst

As I went by the harbour when folk were abed
I saw my dead Lover in his boat pulling in:
My Love he came swiftly and kissed my whitening head,
And my cheeks so hollow and thin.

And face to face we nestled by the wash of the foam,
And after long sorrow the joy it was sweet.
I combed his locks of honey with my little silver comb,
And in my bosom I warmed his feet.

The sea-fog crept round us as white as the wool,
And he lay on the sea-sand with his head on my knee.
No night wind broke the silence nor any shrieking gull,
In that death-white fog from the sea.

And then I crooned him over our sweet songs of old;
Ochone, I could not warm him, and never a word he spoke.
I loosed my heavy hair then, the grey locks with the gold,
And wrapped him in a living cloak.

I never thought to ask him the wherefore he had come,
Or if his heaven were lonely, and this earth so dear;
I prayed with eager longing that the cocks would be dumb
And the night-time last a year.

Ochone, the cocks came crowing, and he arose and went,
His darling black head hanging, out through the sea-fog's snow.
Oh, wherefore, darling, darling, did you break my dull content,
And why did you come but to go?

Oscar Wilde

Silentium Amoris

As often-times the too resplendent sun
Hurries the pallid and reluctant moon
Back to her sombre cave, ere she hath won
A single ballad from the nightingale,
So doth thy Beauty make my lips to fail,
And all my sweetest singing out of tune.

And as at dawn across the level mead
On wings impetuous some wind will come,
And with its too harsh kisses break the reed
Which was its only instrument of song,
So me too stormy passions work my wrong,
And for excess of Love my Love is dumb.

But surely unto Thee mine eyes did show
Why I am silent, and my lute unstrung;
Else it were better we should part, and go,
Thou to some lips of sweeter melody,
And I to nurse the barren memory
Of unkissed kisses, and songs never sung.

Jonathan Swift

Stella's Birthday (1725)

As, when a beauteous nymph decays,
We say, she's past her dancing days;
So, poets lose their feet by time,
And can no longer dance in rhyme.
Your annual bard had rather chose
To celebrate your birth in prose;
Yet, merry folks, who want by chance
A pair to make a country dance,
Call the old housekeeper, and get her
To fill a place, for want of better;
While Sheridan is off the hooks,
And friend Delany at his books,
That Stella may avoid disgrace,
Once more the Dean supplies their place.

Beauty and wit, too sad a truth,
Have always been confined to youth;
The god of wit, and beauty's queen,
He twenty-one, and she fifteen:
No poet ever sweetly sung,
Unless he were like Phoebus, young;
Nor ever nymph inspired to rhyme,

Unless, like Venus, in her prime.
At fifty-six, if this be true,
Am I a poet fit for you?
Or at the age of forty-three,
Are you a subject fit for me?

Adieu bright wit, and radiant eyes;
You must be grave, and I be wise.
Our fate in vain we would oppose,
But I'll be still your friend in prose:
Esteem and friendship to express,
Will not require poetic dress;
And if the muse deny her aid
To have them *sung*, they may be *said*.

But, Stella say, what evil tongue
Reports you are no longer young?
That Time sits with his scythe to mow
Where erst sat Cupid with his bow;

That half your locks are turned to grey;
I'll ne'er believe a word they say.
'Tis true, but let it not be known,
My eyes are somewhat dimmish grown;
For nature, always in the right,
To your decays adapts my sight,
And wrinkles undistinguished pass,

For I'm ashamed to use a glass;
And till I see them with these eyes,
Whoever says you have them, lies.

No length of time can make you quit
Honour and virtue, sense and wit,
Thus you may still be young to me,
While I can better hear than see;
Oh, ne'er may fortune show her spite,
To make me deaf, and mend my sight.

AE

Forgiveness

At dusk the window panes grew grey;
The wet world vanished in the gloom;
The dim and silver end of day
Scarce glittered through the little room.

And all my sins were told; I said
Such things to her who knew not sin—
The sharp ache throbbing in my head,
The fever running high within—

I touched with pain her purity;
Sin's darker sense I could not bring;
My soul was black as night to me;
To her I was a wounded thing.

I needed love no words could say;
She drew me softly nigh her chair,
My head upon her hands to lay,
With cool hands that caressed my hair.

She sat with hands as if to bless
And looked with grave, ethereal eyes,
Ensouled with ancient Quietness
A gentle priestess of the Wise.

EDWARD WALSH

The Dawning of the Day

At early dawn I once had been
Where Lene's blue waters flow,
When summer bid the groves be green,
The lamp of light to glow.
As on by bower, and town, and tower,
And widespread fields I stray,
I meet a maid in the greenwood shade
At the dawning of the day.

Her feet and beauteous head were bare,
No mantle fair she wore;
But down her waist fell golden hair,
That swept the tall grass o'er.
With milking-pail she sought the vale,
And bright her charms' display;
Outshining far the morning star
At the dawning of the day.

Beside me sat that maid divine
Where grassy banks outspread.
'Oh, let me call thee ever mine,
Dear maid,' I sportive said.

'False man, for shame, why bring me blame?'
She cried, and burst away—
The sun's first light pursued her flight
At the dawning of the day.

ULICK O'CONNOR

Oscar Wilde

From the Irish of Brendan Behan

After all the wit
In a sudden fit
Of fear, he skipped it.
Stretched in the twilight
That body once lively
Dumb in the darkness.
Quiet, but for candles
Blazing beside him,
His elegant form
And firm gaze exhausted.
In an empty cold room
With a spiteful concierge
Impatient at waiting
For a foreign master
Who left without paying
The ten per cent service.
Exiled now from Flore
To sanctity's desert
The young prince of Sin
Broken and withered.
Lust left behind him

Gem without lustre
No Pernod for a stiffener
But cold holy water
The young king of Beauty
Narcissus broken.
But the pure star of Mary
As a gleam on the ocean.

ENVOI

Sweet is the way of the sinner
Sad, death without God's praise
My life on you, Oscar boy
Yourself had it both ways.

THOMAS MOORE

At the Mid Hour of Night

At the mid hour of night, when stars are weeping, I fly
To the lone vale we loved, when life shone warm in thine eye;
And I think oft, if spirits can steal from the regions of air,
To revisit past scenes of delight, thou wilt come to me there,
And tell me our love is remembered, even in the sky.

Then I sing the wild song 'twas once such pleasure to hear!
When our voices commingling breath'd, like one, on the ear;
And, as Echo far off through the vale my sad orison rolls,
I think, O my love! 'tis thy voice from the Kingdom of Souls,
Faintly answering still the notes that once were so dear.

JEREMY YOUNG

True Love

Before I fell in love with you

My passion was for philosophic proof,
For metaphysics and theology,

My search was for the esoteric truth,
For inner worlds and hid divinity.

I only saw the truths inside my mind;
My brain was blind

To love's true mystery.

Frank O'Connor

The Unmarried Clergy

FROM THE MIDNIGHT COURT
From the Irish of Brian Merriman

'But oye, my heart will grow grey hairs
Brooding forever on idle cares,
Has the Catholic Church a glimmer of sense
That the priests won't marry like anyone else?
Is it any wonder the way I am,
Out of my mind for the want of a man,
When there's men by the score with looks and leisure,
Walking the roads and scorning pleasure?
The full of a fair of primest beef,
Warranted to afford relief,
Cherry-red cheeks and bull-like voices,
And bellies dripping with fat in slices,
Backs erect and heavy hind quarters,
Hot-blooded men, the best of partners,
Freshness and charm, youth and good looks
And nothing to ease their mind but books!
The best fed men that travel the country,
Beef and mutton, game and poultry,
Whiskey and wine forever in stock,
Sides of bacon, beds of flock.
Mostly they're hardy under the hood,

And we know like ourselves they're flesh and blood;
I wouldn't ask much of the old campaigners,
The good-for-nothings and born complainers,
But petticoat-tossers aloof and idle
And fillies gone wild for bit and bridle!

'Of course I admit that some more sprightly,
Would like to repent and I'd treat them lightly.
A pardon and a job for life
To every cleric that takes a wife!
For many a good man's chance miscarries
If you scuttle the ship for the crooks it carries;
And though some as we know were always savage
Gnashing their teeth at the thought of marriage,
And, modest beyond the needs of merit,
Invoked hell-fire on girls of spirit,
Yet some that took to their pastoral labours
Made very good priests and the best of neighbours.
Many a girl filled byre and stall
And furnished her house through a clerical call.
Everyone's heard of priests extolled
For lonesome women that they consoled;
People I've heard throughout the county
Have nothing but praise for the curate's bounty;
Or uphold the canon to lasting fame
For the children he reared in another man's name;
But I hate to think of their lonely lives,
The passions they waste on middle-aged wives,

While the women they'd choose if the choice were theirs
Go by the wall and comb grey hairs.
It passes the wit of mortal man
What Ireland has lost by this stupid ban.

'I leave it to you, O Nut of Knowledge,
The girls at home and the boys in college,
I'm blest if I can see the crime,
If they go courting in their prime,
But you that for learning have no rival,
Tell us the teachings of the Bible;
Where are we taught to pervert our senses
And make our natural needs offences?
Fly from lust, advised St. Paul,
He didn't mean men to fly us all,
But to leave their father and friends behind
And stick to the girl that pleased their mind.

MÁIRE MHAC AN TSAOI

Finit

From her own Irish poem

By chance I heard about the marriage contract
And thought it strange this check on the wind's lightness
You were as spirited and unpredictable,
As wild as wind and lonely, I remembered.

See how the common lot is yours henceforward,
Hardship and commonplace each following season,
Slid to oblivion as turns the quarter,
We'll doubt you or your like ever existed . . .

But that there'll now be tunes I won't hear ever,
Without you in the corner there appearing,
Waiting, music on hand, before the dance—
Your eyes the mystery of the night outside.

OLIVER ST JOHN GOGARTY

Perfection

By Perfection fooled too long,
I will dream of that no longer;
Venus, you have done me wrong
By your unattainable beauty,
Till it seemed to be my duty
To belittle all the throng.
I have found attraction stronger;
I have found a lady younger
Who can make a hard heart stir:
Like an athlete, tall and slender,
With no more than human splendour;
Yet, for all the faults of her,
Than Perfection perfecter.

Though she guards it, grace breaks through
Every blithe and careless movement;
What shall I compare her to?
When she takes the ball left-handed,
Speed and sweetness are so blended
Nothing awkward she can do,
She, whose faults are an improvement!
If she only knew what Love meant
I would not be seeking now

To describe the curved perfection
Of all loveliness in action—
Perfect she would be, I vow,
With the mole above the brow!

F. R. Higgins

By the Field of the Crab-Trees

By the field of the crab-trees my love and I were walking
And talking most sweetly to each other;
In the three-cornered field, we walked in early autumn,
And these were the words of my lover.
And softly, softly, his words were moving through me—
Coaxing as a fife, crying as a fiddle—
That I heard my heart beat, as dew beats on the stubble;
And the twilight was then lying with us.

ALFRED ALLEN

Love and the Years

Can love exist without mortality?
Can I adore a quite unchanging face?
How can I, when what binds my love to me
Is woven strand by strand of fickle days?

And by this constant change more constant is
Than any love for an undying God
Can ever be; for how can mortal eyes
Distinguish the Immortal from the Dead?

Indeed the love for what has always been
Turns to indifference outside of time,
Cupped in the hand of silence, rapt, alone,
Ridiculous to me, because sublime.

Love is a thing that's gathered, chance by chance,
Out of life's ever-changing random dance.

George Farquhar

Song from The Recruiting Officer

Come, fair one, be kind
You never shall find
A fellow so fit for a lover:
The world shall view
My passion for you,
But never your passion discover.

I still will complain
Of your frowns and disdain
Though I revel through all your charms:
The world shall declare,
That I die with despair,
When I only die in your arms.

I still will adore,
And love more and more,
But, by Jove, if you chance to prove cruel:
I'll get me a miss
That freely will kiss,
Though I afterwards drink water-gruel.

JAMES STEPHENS

The Coolin

Come with me, under my coat,
And we will drink our fill
Of the milk of the white goat,
Or wine if it be thy will

And we will talk, until
Talk is a trouble, too,
Out on the side of the hill;
And nothing is left to do,

But an eye to look into an eye;
And a hand in a hand to slip;
And a sigh to answer a sigh;
And a lip to find out a lip!

What if the night be black!
Or the air on the mountain chill!
Where the goat lies down in her track,
And all but the fern is still!

Stay with me, under my coat!
And we will drink our fill
Of the milk of the white goat,
Out on the side of the hill!

Anonymous

The Humble Petition of a Beautiful Young Lady

To the Reverend Doctor B-rK—y

Dear Doctor, here comes a young virgin untainted
To your Shrine at Bermudas to be married and sainted;
I am young, I am soft, I am blooming and tender,
Of all that I have I make you a surrender;
My innocence led by the voice of your fame
To your person and virtue must put in its claim:
And now I behold you, I truly believe
That you're as like Adam, as I am like Eve:
Before the dire serpent their virtue betrayed.
And taught them to fly from the sun to the shade;
But you, as in you a new race has begun,
Are teaching to fly from the shade to the sun;
For you, in great goodness, your friends are persuading
To go, and to live, and be wise in your Eden.
Oh! let me go with you, oh! pity my youth,
Oh! take me from hence, let me not lose my truth;
Sure you that have virtue so much on your mind
Can't think to leave me, who am virtue, behind;
If you make me your wife, Sir, in time you may fill a
Whole town with your children, and likewise your villa;
I famous for breeding, you famous for knowledge,

I'll found a whole nation, you'll found a whole college.
When many long ages in joys we have spent,
Our souls we'll resign with utmost content;
And gently we'll sink beneath cypress and yew,
You lying by me, and I lying by you.

Sir Samuel Ferguson

The Lark in the Clear Air

Dear thoughts are in my mind
And my soul soars enchanted,
As I hear the sweet lark sing
In the clear air of the day.
For a tender beaming smile
To my hope has been granted,
And tomorrow she shall hear
All my fond heart would say.

I shall tell her all my love,
All my soul's adoration;
And I think she will hear me
And will not say me nay.
It is this that fills my soul
With its joyous elation,
As I hear the sweet lark sing
In the clear air of the day.

THEO DORGAN

Death Will Come

Death will come and have your eyes
and I will go into her arms
without fear or hesitation.

Frost on the slates
of our beloved square,
the cars riding low under
a hurrying sky when

I open the great hall-door
and take her hand,
her long black coat.

The bare-flagged hallway, frost
and perfume on the night air.

I watch her let down
her gleaming hair,
open her slender arms
in your exact gesture.

Death will come and have your eyes
and I will go into her arms
without fear or hesitation.

George Moore

Rondo

Did I love thee? I only did desire
To hold thy body unto mine,
And smite it with strange fire
Of kisses burning as a wine,
And catch thy odorous hair, and twine
It through my fingers amorously.
Did I love thee?

Did I love thee? I only did desire
To drink the perfume of thy blood
In vision, and thy senses tire
Seeing them shift from ebb to flood
In consonant sweet interlude,
And if love such a thing not be,
I loved not thee.

Brendan Kennelly

Reconciliation

From the sixteenth-century Irish

Do not torment me, woman,
Let our two minds be as one,
Be my mate in my own land
Where we may live till life is done.

Put your mouth against my mouth
You whose skin is fresh as foam,
Take me in your white embrace
And let us love till kingdom come.

Slender graceful girl, admit
Me soon into your bed,
Discord, pain will disappear
When we stretch there side by side.

For your sweet sake, I will ignore
Every girl who takes my eye,
If it's possible, I implore
You do the same for me.

As I have given from my heart
Passion for which alone I live,
Let me now receive from you
The love you have to give.

MARY TWOMEY

Exchanges in Italy

Do you remember
how I made you sit
as still as marble
with closed eyes?
Festooned you with
grapes and apricots
a peach in either
outstretched hand
pomegranates on
your knees
green leaves
in your hair?
There was a straw
Chianti at your feet.
We drank straight
from the bottle.

Morning . . . we
watched the jewellers
on the Ponte Vecchio
unpadlock their shutters
nail-studded like
dungeon doors.

I still wear the
ring you gave me
made of string.

You showed me goblets
of lapis lazuli
vases of rock crystal
with silver lips.
We walked through
cool dark tunnels
of ilex and cypress.
Lizards lay motionless
on hot dry stones.
Heat rose, fierce
and tremulous.

When at last
I did allow
you to speak,
your words were
chalcedony and
pearl that I
have hoarded
to myself.

EUGENE O'CURRY

Do You Remember That Night?

From the Irish

Do you remember that night
When you were at the window,
With neither hat nor gloves
Nor coat to shelter you?
I reached out my hand to you,
And you ardently grasped it;
I remained to converse with you
Until the lark began to sing.

Do you remember that night
That you and I were
At the foot of the rowan tree,
And the night drifting snow?
Your head on my breast,
And your pipe sweetly playing?
Little thought I that night
That our love ties would loosen!

Beloved of my inmost heart,
Come some night and soon,
When my people are at rest,

That we may talk together.
My arms shall encircle you
While I relate my sad tale,
That your soft, pleasant converse
Hath deprived me of heaven.

The fire is unraked,
The light unextinguished,
The key under the door,
Do you softly draw it.
My mother is asleep,
But I am wide awake;
My fortune in my hand,
I am ready to go with you.

WILLIAM CONGREVE

Fair Amoret

Fair Amoret is gone astray;
Pursue and seek her, every Lover;
I'll tell the signs, by which you may
The wandering shepherdess discover.

Coquet and coy at once her air,
Both studied though both seem neglected;
Careless she is with artful care,
Affecting to seem unaffected.

With skill her eyes dart every glance,
Yet change so soon you'd ne'er suspect 'em;
For she'd persuade they wound by chance,
Though certain aim and art direct 'em.

She likes her self, yet others hates
For that which in her self she prizes;
And while she laughs at them, forgets
She is the thing that she despises.

ROBIN FLOWER

At Parting

From the Irish

False love, since thou and I must sever,
Hear this, the swansong of my passion,
Let us be twain henceforth forever,
Let thy heart follow my heart's fashion,

If thou shalt hear man speak about me,
If low or high scorn or befriend me,
Then leave them thou to praise or flout me,
Neither revile nor defend me,

And if in church or cell thou beest,
In field enclosed or open meadow,
Whate'er I see, whate'er thou seest,
Let's turn each from the other's shadow.

Speak not, and I will speak them never,
Love-names or names our fathers gave us;
Forget as I forget forever
How love with looking did enslave us.

MYLES DILLON

Farewell to Last Night

From the Irish of Niall More Mac Murray

Farewell to last night!
The memory will not fade.
Though I were to die for it,
I wish that it were beginning now.

There are two in this house tonight
whose eyes cannot hide their secret;
though they are not mouth to mouth,
each looks with longing at the other.

Silence gives meaning
to the language of the eyes;
and silence of the lips cannot keep
the secret that a glance betrays.

Ah, gentle eyes, the slanderers of love
have sealed my lips.
Watch what my eyes are saying,
as you sit over there:

'Keep night around us!
Would that we could stay like this for ever!
Do not let morning in!
Arise and put out the light of day!'

Ah, Mary, gracious mother,
queen of scholars, come and take me
by the hand—Farewell to last night!

Tom MacIntyre

On Sweet Killen Hill

From the Irish

Flower of the flock,
Any time, any land,
Plenty your ringlets,
Plenty your hand,
Sunlight your window,
Laughter your sill,
And I must be with you
On sweet Killen Hill.

Let sleep renegue me,
Skin lap my bones,
Love and tomorrow
Can handle the reins,
You my companion
I'd never breathe ill,
And I guarantee bounty
On sweet Killen Hill.

You'll hear the pack yell
As puss devil-dances,
Hear cuckoo and thrush

Pluck song from the branches,
See fish in the pool
Doing their thing,
And the bay as God made it
From sweet Killen Hill.

Pulse of my life,
We come back to—*Mise*.
Why slave for McArdle,
That bumbailiff's issue?
I've a harp in a thousand,
Love songs at will,
And the air is cadenza
On sweet Killen Hill.

Gentle one, lovely one,
Come to me,
Now sleep the clergy,
Now sleep their care,
Sunrise will find us
But sunrise won't tell
That love lacks surveillance
On sweet Killen Hill.

AUSTIN CLARKE

Flower-Quiet in the Rush-Strewn Sheiling

Flower-quiet in the rush-strewn sheiling
At the dawntime Grainne lay,
While beneath the birch-toppled roof the sunlight
Groped upon its way
And stooped over her sleeping white body
With a wasp-yellow ray.

The hot breath of the day awoke her,
And wearied of its heat
She wandered out by noisy elms
On the cool mossy peat,
Where the shadowed leaves like pecking linnets
Nodded around her feet.

She leaned and saw in pale grey waters,
By twisted hazel boughs,
Her lips like heavy drooping poppies
In a rich redness drowse,
Then swallow-lightly touched the ripples
Until her wet lips were
Burning as ripened rowan berries
Through the white winter air.

Lazily she lingered
Gazing so,
As the slender osiers
Where the waters flow,
As green twigs of sally
Swaying to and fro.
Sleepy moths fluttered
In her dark eyes,
And her lips grew quieter
Than lullabies.
Swaying with the reedgrass
Over the stream
Lazily she lingered
Cradling a dream.

A brown bird rises
Out of the marshes,
By sallow pools flying
On winds from the sea,
By pebbly rivers,
Tired of the salt gusts
Sweetly 'twill whistle
On a mountainy tree.
So, gladdened, impulsive,
Grainne arising
Sped through the bluebells
Under the branches,
White by the alders

Glimmering she
Stole in the shadows,
Flashing through sunshine,
Her feet like the raindrops
On withered leaves falling
Lightful and free.

She stood beyond the reddening hawthorns
Out in the wild air
And gathering back with white-lit fingers
Her wind-loosened hair,
She scanned the dark bog-waters
Sleeping beneath the bare
Turf banks and the wide brown marshes,
But she could only find
The froth-pale blossom of the boglands
As it fluttered on the waves of the wandering wind
So she came, a little saddened,
Bending with the slim breeze
Through the elm-misted sunshine
And flowers like pools of blue seas.
Quiet as her breath she glided,
In the grass-green shade of trees.

A bird sang like a rainy well,
Then on a fallen bough
A hurrying footstep spoke, and Diarmuid
Stood before her now,
Sunburnt, pine-straight, the hilly breezes
Upon his lips and brow.

MAURICE JAMES CRAIG

Love Poem

Flowers upon your lips and hands,
The gentle movement of your breast:
I have remembered these in lands
Where I was but a passing guest.

Strange, to have seen so long before,
Reflected through each flow and fault,
This inlet on the sunlit shore
Where the sweet water meets the salt.

Michael Longley

In Mayo

I

For her sake once again I disinter
Imagination like a brittle skull
From where the separating vertebrae
And scapulae litter a sandy wind,

As though to reach her I must circle
This burial mound, its shadow turning
Under the shadow of a seabird's wing:
A sundial for the unhallowed soul.

II

Though the townland's all ears, all eyes
To decipher our movements, she and I
Appear on the scene at the oddest times:
We follow the footprints of animals,

Then vanish into the old wives' tales
Leaving behind us landmarks to be named
After our episodes, and the mushrooms
That cluster where we happen to lie.

III

When it is time for her to fall asleep
And I touch her eyelids, may night itself,
By my rule of thumb, be no profounder
Than the grassy well among irises

Where wild duck shelter their candid eggs:
No more beguiling than a gull's feather
In whose manifold gradations of light
I clothe her now and erase the scene.

IV

Dawns and dusks here should consist of
Me scooping a hollow for her hip-bone,
The stony headland a bullaun, a cup
To balance her body in like water:

Then a slow awakening to the swans
That fly home in twos, married for life,
Larks nestling beside the cattle's feet
And snipe the weight of the human soul.

Douglas Hyde

I Shall Not Die for Thee

For thee I shall not die,
Woman high of fame and name;
Foolish men thou mayest slay
I and they are not the same.

Why should I expire
For the fire of any eye,
Slender waist or swan-like limb,
Is't for them that I should die?

The round breasts, the fresh skin,
Cheeks crimson, hair so long and rich;
Indeed, indeed, I shall not die,
Please God, not I, for any such.

The golden hair, the forehead thin,
The chaste mien, the gracious ease,
The rounded heel, the languid tone,
Fools alone find death from these.

Thy sharp wit, thy perfect calm,
Thy thin palm like foam of sea;

Thy white neck, thy blue eye,
I shall not die for thee.

Woman, graceful as the swan,
A wise man did nurture me,
Little palm, white neck, bright eye,
I shall not die for ye.

SIR RICHARD STEELE

The Love-Sick Maid

From place to place forlorn I go,
With downcast eyes a silent shade:
Forbidden to declare my woe;
To speak, till spoken to, afraid.

My inward pangs, my secret grief,
My soft consenting looks betray:
He loves, but gives me no relief:
Why speaks not he who may?

EAVAN BOLAND

Ready for Flight

From this I will not swerve nor fall nor falter:
If around your heart the crowds disperse
And I who at their whim now freeze or swelter
Am allowed to come to a more temperate place,

And if a runner starts to run to me
Dispatched by you, crying that all is trampled
Under foot, terraces smashed, the entry
Into holy places rudely sampled,

Then I would come at once my love with love
Bringing to wasted areas the sight
Of butterfly and swan and turtle dove
Their wings ruffled like snails ready for flight.
In such surroundings, after the decease
Of devils, you and I would live in peace.

RICHARD BRINSLEY SHERIDAN

Song

Give Isaac the nymph who no beauty can boast;
But health and good humour to make her his toast,
If strait, I don't mind whether slender or fat,
And six feet or four—we'll ne'er quarrel for that.

Whate'er her complexion, I vow I don't care,
If brown it is lasting, more pleasing if fair;
And tho' in her cheeks I no dimples should see,
Let her smile, and each dell is a dimple to me.

Let her locks be the reddest that ever were seen,
And her eyes may be e'en any colour but green,
For in eyes, tho' so various in lustre and hue,
I swear I've no choice, only let her have two.

'Tis true I'd dispense with a throne on her back,
And white teeth I own, are genteeler than black,
A little round chin too's a beauty I've heard,
But I only desire she mayn't have a beard.

Edward Lysaght

Garnyvillo

Have you been at Garnyvillo?
Have you seen at Garnyvillo
Beauty's train trip o'er the plain
With lovely Kate of Garnyvillo?
Oh! she's pure as virgin snows,
Ere they light on woodland hill-O;
Sweet as dew-drop on wild rose,
Is lovely Kate of Garnyvillo!

Philomel, I've listen'd oft
To thy lay, nigh weeping willow—
Oh, the strain's more sweet, more soft,
That flows from Kate of Garnyvillo!
Have you been, etc.

As a noble ship I've seen
Sailing o'er the swelling billow,
So I've marked the graceful mien
Of lovely Kate of Garnyvillo.
Have you been, etc.

If poets' prayers can banish cares,
No cares should come to Garnyvillo;

Joy's bright rays shall gild her days,
And dove-like peace perch on her pillow:
Charming maid of Garnyvillo!
Lovely maid of Garnyvillo!
Beauty, grace, and virtue wait
On lovely Kate of Garnyvillo!

Brendan Kennelly

Love-Cry

He mounted her, growing between her thighs.
A mile away, the Shannon swelled and thrust
Into the sea, ignoring the gaunt curlew-cries.
Near where the children played in gathering dusk
John Martin Connor cocked his polished gun
And fired at plover over Nolan's hill;
A second late, he shot the dying sun
And swore at such an unrewarding kill.

A quick voice called, one child turned and ran,
Somewhere in Brandon's river a trout leaped,
Infinite circles made nightspirits stare;
The hunter tensed, the birds approached again
As though they had a binding tryst to keep.
Her love-cry thrilled and perished on the air.

JOSEPH CAMPBELL

Sighle of the Lovespot

He praised my breasts so round and white,
My amber hair, my eyes of light,
My singlet without stain or speck,
The little lovespot on my neck.

He gave me cordwain shoes to wear,
And ribbands for my neck and hair;
And then he took his will of me,
And went away beyond the sea.

He told me he would come again,
With silver and a sword of Spain;
But now it is the pride o' the year,
And Art Ó Lúinigh is not here.

I'll make a bed on Eithne's stone,
And lay me down to sleep, alone:
I would not weep, I would not chide,
If only he lay by my side.

Would God the beard was on the corn.
Would God my silly babe was born,
Would God the nuts were in the trees,
And this poor heart might feel at ease!

PAUL DURCAN

Martha's Wall

Her pleasure—what gave her pleasure—was to be walked
Down her wall, the South Wall, a skinny, crinkly, golden-stemmed wall
That contracts and expands, worms and unworms, in and out of Dublin Bay
Across the sea's thighs pillowing in, besotted, under daisy-gartered skies.
She'd curl her finger around my finger and I'd lead her out on to it.
She liked it when the flowering sea was shedding spray across it.
She'd tense up with delight to see me get wet
And wetter still, and wetter—the wetter it was
The better she liked it, and me—and she wanted always
To get down, away down, to the very end of it
Where there is a deep-red lighthouse, and the deep-red lighthouse
Was hers also, hers, and we'd sit down on a bench under it
And she'd put her arm around my neck and we'd stop needing to speak
And we'd sit there, breathless, in silence, for a long time.

Richard Brinsley Sheridan

Song

Here's to the maiden of bashful fifteen;
Here's to the widow of fifty;
Here's to the flaunting extravagant quean,
And here's to the housewife that's thrifty.
Chorus.
Let the toast pass,—
Drink to the lass,
I'll warrant she'll prove an excuse for the glass.

Here's to the charmer whose dimples we prize;
Now to the maid who has none, sir:
Here's to the girl with a pair of blue eyes,
And here's to the nymph with but *one*, sir.
Chorus. Let the toast pass, &c.

Here's to the maid with a bosom of snow;
Now to her that's as brown as a berry:
Here's to the wife with a face full of woe,
And now to the girl that is merry.
Chorus. Let the toast pass, &c.

For let 'em be clumsy, or let 'em be slim,
Young or ancient, I care not a feather;
So fill a pint bumper quite up to the brim,
And let us e'en toast them together.
Chorus. Let the toast pass, &c.

Jane, Lady Wilde ('Speranza')

Corinne's Last Love-Song

I

How beautiful, how beautiful you streamed upon my sight,
In glory and in grandeur, as a gorgeous sunset-light!
How softly, soul-subduing, fell your words upon mine ear,
Like low aerial music when some angel hovers near!
What tremulous, faint ecstacy to clasp your hand in mine,
Till the darkness fell upon me of a glory too divine!
The air around grew languid with our intermingled breath,
And in your beauty's shadow I sank motionless as death.
I saw you not, I heard not, for a mist was on my brain—
I only felt that life could give no joy like that again.

II

And this was Love—I knew it not, but blindly floated on,
And now I'm on the ocean waste, dark, desolate, alone;
The waves are raging round me—I'm reckless where they guide;
No hope is left to light me, no strength to stem the tide.
As a leaf along the torrent, a cloud across the sky,
As dust upon the whirlwind, so my life is drifting by.
The dream that drank the meteor's light—the form from Heav'n has
    flown—
The vision and the glory, they are passing—they are gone.
Oh! love is frantic agony, and life one throb of pain;
Yet I would bear its darkest woes to dream that dream again.

ROBIN FLOWER

The Proud Lady

From the Irish of Gerald Fitzgerald, 4th Earl of Desmond

How far apart are she and I!
I and the lady of my heart;
I yearn in love; she passes by
Too proud one kind word to impart.

For gold she left me here to moan,
Gold set her fragile thought astray;
But, came she in her shift along,
I'd take her to my heart today.

How lightly on her spirit lies
The love that crushes my poor heart!
And, ah, she mocks my miseries
How far are she and I apart!

John Hewitt

From Sonnets for Roberta

How have I served you? I have let you waste
the substance of your summer on my mood;
the image of the woman is defaced,
and some mere chattel-thing of cloth and wood
performs the household rites, while I, content,
mesh the fine words to net the turning thought,
or eke the hours out, gravely diligent,
to draw to sight that which, when it is brought,
is seldom worth the labour, while you wait
the little loving gestures held at bay,
each mocking moment inappropriate
for pompous duty never stoops to play;
Yet, sometimes, at a pause, I recognise
the lonely pity in your lifted eyes.

GEORGE SIGERSON

Love's Despair

From the Irish of Dermot O'Curran

I am desolate,
Bereft by bitter fate;
No cure beneath the skies can save me,
No cure on sea or strand,
Nor in any human hand—
But hers, this paining wound who gave me.

I know not night from day,
Nor thrush from cuckoo grey,
Nor cloud from the sun that shines above thee—
Nor freezing cold from heat,
Nor friend—if friend I meet—
I but know—heart's love!—I love thee.

Love that my Life began,
Love, that will close life's span,
Love that grows ever by love-giving:
Love, from the first to last,
Love, till all life be passed,
Love that loves on after living!

This love I gave to thee,
For pain love has given me,
Love that can fail or falter never—
But, spite of earth above,
Guards thee, my Flower of love,
Thou marvel-maid of life for ever.

Bear all things evidence,
Thou art my very sense,
My past, my present, and my morrow!
All else on earth is crossed,
All in the world is lost—
Lost all—but the great love-gift of sorrow.

My life not life, but death;
My voice not voice—a breath;
No sleep, no quiet—thinking ever
On thy fair phantom face,
Queen eyes and royal grace,
Lost loveliness that leaves me never.

I pray thee grant but this—
From thy dear mouth one kiss,
That the pang of death-despair pass over:
Or bid make ready nigh
The place where I shall lie,
For aye, thy leal and silent lover.

The Earl of Longford

The Careful Husband

From the Irish

I am told, sir, you're keeping an eye on your wife,
But I can't see the reason for that, on my life.
For if you go out, O most careful of men,
It is clear that you can't keep an eye on her then.

Even when you're at home and take every care,
It is only a waste of your trouble, I swear.
For if you for one instant away from her look,
She'll be off into some inaccessible nook.

If you sit close beside her and don't let her move,
By the flick of an eyelid she'll signal her love.
If you keep her in front of you under your eye,
She will do what she likes and your caution defy.

When she goes out to Mass, as she'd have you suppose,
You must not stay a minute, but go where she goes.
You must not walk in front nor yet too far behind her.
But she's got such a start that I doubt if you'll find her.

MICHAEL HARTNETT

I Cannot Lie Here Anymore . . .

From the Irish of Nuala Ní Dhomhnaill

I cannot lie here anymore
in your aroma—
with your pillowed mouth
asnore,
your idle hand
across my hip
not really caring
whether I exist

I'm not upset
because you ignore me
nor because our happy summer
washes over me—
it's not the bedside flowers
that intoxicate
but your body, your aroma
a blend of blood and earth.

I'll get up from the bed
And put on my clothes
and leave with the car keys

from your fist stolen
and drive to the city

At nine tomorrow
you'll get a call
telling you where to go
to pick up your car—
but I cannot lie anymore
where your aroma laps—
because I'll fall in love with you,
(perhaps)

JAMES GLEASHURE

From Mary Hogan's Quatrains

From the Irish

II

I care little for people's suspicions,
I care little for priests' prohibitions,
For anything save to lie stretched
Between you and the wall—

I am indifferent to the night's cold
I am indifferent to the squall or rain,
When in this warm narrow secret world
Which does not go beyond the edge of the bed—

We shall not contemplate what lies before us,
What already has been done,
Time is on our side, my dearest,
And it will last till morning.

VI

Tonight seems never ending!
There was once a night

Which with you was not long—
Dare I call to mind

That would not be hard, for sure,
The road on which I would return—
If it were permitted
After repentance

Lying down for enjoyment
And rising for pleasure
That is what we practised—
If only I could return to it.

Thomas MacGreevy

Dechtire

I do not love you as I loved
The loves I have loved,
As I may love others:

I know you are not beautiful
As some I loved were beautiful,
As others may be:

I do not hold your counsel dear
As I've held others,
As I still hold some:

And yet
There is no truth but you,
No beauty but you,
No love but you—

And Oh! there is no pain
But you and me.

Thomas MacDonagh

John-John

I dreamt last night of you, John-John,
And thought you called to me;
And when I woke this morning, John,
Yourself I hoped to see;
But I was all alone, John-John,
Though still I heard your call:
I put my boots and bonnet on,
And took my Sunday shawl,
And went, full sure to find you, John,
To Nenagh fair.

The fair was just the same as then,
Five years ago to-day,
When first you left the thimble men
And came with me away;
For there again were thimble men
And shooting galleries,
And card-trick men and Maggie men
Of all sorts and degrees—
But not a sight of you, John-John,
Was anywhere.

I turned my face to home again,
And called myself a fool
To think you'd leave the thimble men
And live again by rule,
And go to Mass and keep the fast
And till the little patch:
My wish to have you home was past
Before I raised the latch
And pushed the door and saw you, John,
Sitting down there.

How cool you came in here, begad,
As if you owned the place!
But rest yourself there now, my lad,
'Tis good to see your face;
My dream is out, and now by it
I think I know my mind;
At six o'clock this house you'll quit,
And leave no grief behind;—
But until six o'clock, John-John,
My bit you'll share

The neighbours' shame of me began
When first I brought you in
To wed and keep a tinker man
They thought a kind of sin;

But now this three year since you're gone
'Tis pity me they do,
And that I'd rather have, John-John,
Than that they'd pity you.
Pity for me and you, John-John,
I could not bear.

Oh, you're my husband right enough,
But what's the good of that?
You know you never were the stuff
To be the cottage cat,
To watch the fire and hear me lock
The door and put out Shep—
But there now, it is six o'clock
And time for you to step.
God bless and keep you far, John-John!
And that's my prayer.

Dermot Bolger

From the Lament for Arthur Cleary

I drifted into sleep
To see a horse come riderless
Over fields trailing
A bridle smeared with blood

Towards a white house
Where a woman stood screaming
As I shuddered awake
I realised her voice was mine

I ran into the street
Where small clusters gathered
Whose eyes avoided me
When I raced frantically past

Guided by the silence
To the narrow tumbledown lane
In which singing blades
Had ended their intimate work

I knew they'd get you
Down some alleyway like that

Ringed by silent gangs
With both the exits blocked

You never knew fear
And that caused your death
Trusting the familiar
You roared into their trap

You'd become an exile
Caught in your native city
Whose police eyed you
Distrustful of neutrality

The dealers watched
Hating your open contempt
And kids growing up
Dreamt of your motor bike

Secretly dismantled
For new needles and deals
They hovered waiting
Every morning you left me

One Friday a lender
Arrived menacing at our flat
Hunting a neighbour
You grabbed his black folder

Releasing the pages
To scatter down into the yard
Like fugitive planets
From an exploding white star

That would eclipse us
Within its relentless orbit
I watched loose pages
Flutter into death warrants

That you just ignored
In sleep I saw charred corpses
I could not recognise
And clutched you till you woke

Begging you to leave
Now while we still might escape
You smiled back at me
Listening to late night traffic

And said in wonderment
My love I have finally come home
Then curled against me
As if love could save us from harm

My lament for you Arthur Cleary
And for the life which we led
For your laughter given freely
From those blood stained lips

In that year we lived as one
Without priest or registrar
To bless the ringlets of sweat
That tied our limbs together

I will not put on black
And spin out my life in mourning
I will breathe your name
On the lips of another's children

Like a secretive tongue
They will carry in their hearts
To the foreign factories
In which their lives will pass

When loud sirens scream
Across the European continent
And they walk into dawn
Towards scrubbed dormitories

They will tell the fable
Of the one who tried to return
And ride a glinting bike
In a final gesture of freedom

And think of early light
Slanted down that crooked lane
When their ancestor fell
And the new enslavement began

Austin Clarke

Gracey Nugent

From the Irish

I drink, wherever I go, to the charms
Of Gracey Nugent in whose white arms
I dare not look for more. Enraptured
By a kiss or two, a little slap,
Her virtue cannot harm me.

Delightful to share her company
Even with others. While she is speaking,
Music goes by and what she smiles at,
Would bring the swan back to the tide.
Was ever plight so pleasing?

Her graceful walk, her pearly neck-lace,
And bosom so near, have made me reckless.
I want to sit, clasping her waist,
Upon her boudoir sofa, waste
Hope. Days are only seconds.

Happy the young fellow, who wins
And can enjoy her without sinning.
Close in the darkness, they will rest
Together and when her fears are less,
She'll take his meaning in

And know at last why he is seeking
Shoulder and breast, her shapely cheeks,
All that I must not try to sing of.
The modest may not point a finger
Or mention what is best.

And so I raise my glass, content
To drink a health to Gracey Nugent,
Her absence circles around the table.
Empty the rummer while you are able,
Two Sundays before Lent

SIOBHÁN CAMPBELL

The Chairmaker

I have been tempted to rush the job
to cut, not shave; to glue, not join
but when I stand beside it
and it's a friend or when I sit astride
and it's solid as a past, then I know
I am right to bide my time.

When people ask me how, I say
'My lady knows, she bakes loaves of bread.'
I tried that too until she said
if I kept opening the oven door
her rise would fall.

So I went back out to my shed
and dreamt myself a piece of elm.
I watched its wave and fingered its swell
and started to work slow as you like
letting my bevel follow the grain.

But this straight back kept coming up long
thinned as it came until almost a pole.
I kept going although it was strange,
honing the shaft and slatting the seat
which was high and tiny and more like a tray.

She came to me when the loaves were done
as if to make up for forcing me out.
She looked at it and her eyes were lit,
'A bird table! We can put it outside,
sit on your chairs and watch them sing.'
And eat your bread, I said, (I felt obliged)
and that night was as good as it's ever been.

EITHNE STRONG

A Farewell

I have not won
until I speak my words.
There is residual tide that must outflow
to leave me quiet abrood.

Good-bye my love.
Indeed it seemed you were my love
that first upon the evening sands
I looked into your darkening eyes:
But still I'll say good-bye.

Good-bye for me
who came from out my tangled ways
to set about you all my dream until the end.
But still I'll say good-bye.

Good-bye dear love
who are and who are not.
The bitter binding must undo
that life may flow its untold course.
You must be free to find your peace
and I, to know my own.
And so good-bye.

The dream that was I've told to go.
Yet bleeding tears will drip within
and dream of mine in brown bog lie
beneath the earth
forever, so good-bye, good-bye.

James Joyce

XXXVI

I hear an army charging upon the land,
And the thunder of horses plunging, foam about their knees:
Arrogant, in black armour, behind them stand,
Disdaining the reins, with fluttering whips, the charioteers.

They cry unto the night their battle-name:
I moan in sleep when I hear afar their whirling laughter.
They cleave the gloom of dreams, a blinding flame,
Clanging, clanging upon the heart as upon an anvil.

They come shaking in triumph their long, green hair:
They come out of the sea and run shouting by the shore.
My heart, have you no wisdom thus to despair?
My love, my love, my love, why have you left me alone?

Derek Mahon

The Old Snaps

I keep your old snaps in my bottom drawer—
The icons of a more than personal love.
Look, three sisters out of Chekhov
('When will we ever go to Moscow?')
Ranged on the steps of the school-house
Where their mother is head teacher,
Out on the rocks, or holding down their hair
In a high wind on a North Antrim shore.
Later, yourself alone among sand-hills
Striking a slightly fictional pose,
Life-ready and impervious to harm
In your wind-blown school uniform,
While the salt sea air fills
Your young body with ozone
And fine sand trickles into your shoes.
I think I must have known you even then.

We went to Moscow, and we will again;
Meanwhile we walk on the strand
And smile as if for the first time
While the children play in the sand.

We have never known a worse winter
But the old snaps are always there
Framed for ever in your heart and mine
Where no malicious hands can twist or tear.

Anonymous

I Know Where I'm Going

I know where I'm goin';
And I know who's goin' with me,
I know who I love,
But the dear knows who I'll marry!

I have stockings of silk,
Shoes of fine green leather,
Combs to buckle my hair,
And a ring for every finger.

I have treasures of gold,
In my heart all hidden;
Only my grief untold,
And a trembling tear unbidden.

Feather beds are soft,
And painted rooms are bonny,
But I would leave them all
To go with my love Johnny.

Strangers pass me by
In this world I'm lonely,
For my Johnny I sigh,
For 'tis him that I love only.

Some say he is dark
But I say he's bonny,
The bravest of them all
My handsome winning Johnny.

I know where I'm goin'
And I know who's goin' with me,
I know who I love,
But the dear knows who I'll marry!

Eavan Boland

The Other Woman

For Kevin

I know you have a world I cannot share
Where a woman waits for you, beautiful,
Young no doubt, protected in your care
From stiffening and wrinkling, not mortal

Not shy of her own mirror. How can I rival
Her when like a harem wife she waits
To come into the pages of your novel
Obediently as if to your bed on nights

She is invited, not as in your other life
I do, reminds you daily of the defeat
Of time, nor as does your other wife,
Binds you to the married state.

She is the other woman. I must share
You with her time and time again,
Book after book, yet I am aware
Love, how I have got the better bargain

For I imagine she has grown strange

To you among the syntax and the sentences

By which you distance her and would exchange

Her speaking part for any of our silences.

EDWARD DOWDEN

The Plummet

I let my plummet sink and sink
Into this sea of blessing; when,
Or where should it touch shoal? I think
Love lies beyond our furthest ken.

Above, the sun-smit waves career;
They have their voices wild and free;
Below them, where no eye can peer,
Love's great glad taciturnity.

LADY GREGORY

The Enchanted Mistress

From the Irish of Aodhagán O'Rathaille [Egan O'Rahilly]

I met brightness of brightness upon the path of loneliness;
Plaiting of plaiting in every lock of her yellow hair.
News of news she gave me, and she as lonely as she was;
News of the coming back of him that owns the tribute of the king.

Folly of follies I to go so near to her,
Slave I was made by a slave that put me in hard bonds.
She made away from me then and I following after her
Till we came to a house of houses made by Druid enchantments.

They broke into mocking laughter, a troop of men of enchantments,
And a troop of young girls with smooth-plaited hair.
They put me up in chains, they made no delay about it—
And my love holding to her breast an awkward ugly clown.

I told her then with the truest words I could tell her,
It was not right for her to be joined with a common clumsy churl;
And the man that was three times fairer than the whole race of the Scots
Waiting till she would come to him to be his beautiful bride.

At the sound of my words her pride set her crying,
The tears were running down over the kindling of her cheeks.
She sent a lad to bring me safe from the place I was in.
She is the brightness of brightness I met in the path of loneliness.

Paul Durcan

Nessa

I met her on the First of August
In the Shangri-La Hotel,
She took me by the index finger
And dropped me in her well.
And that was a whirlpool, that was a whirlpool,
And I very nearly drowned.

Take off your pants, she said to me,
And I very nearly didn't;
Would you care to swim, she said to me,
And I hopped into the Irish sea.
And that was a whirlpool, that was a whirlpool,
And I very nearly drowned.

On the way back I fell in the field
And she fell down beside me.
I'd have lain in the grass with her all my life
With Nessa:
She was a whirlpool, she was a whirlpool,
And I very nearly drowned.

Oh Nessa my dear, Nessa my dear,
Will you stay with me on the rocks?

Will you come for me into the Irish sea
And for me let your red hair down?
And then we will ride into Dublin city
In a taxi-cab wrapped-up in dust.
Oh you are a whirlpool, you are a whirlpool,
And I am very nearly drowned.

THOMAS MOORE

Ode to Nea

Written at Bermuda . . . Tale iter omne cave.

PROPERTIUS IV, ELEGY 8

I pray you, let us roam no more
Along that wild and lonely shore,
Where late we thoughtless strayed;
'Twas not for us, whom Heaven intends
To be no more than simple friends,
Such lonely walks were made.

That little bay where, winding in
From Ocean's rude and angry din
(As lovers steal to bliss),
The billows kiss the shore, and then
Flow calmly to the deep again,
As though they did not kiss!

Remember, o'er its circling flood
In what a dangerous dream we stood—
The silent sea before us,
Around us, all the gloom of grove,
That e'er was spread for guilt or love,
No eye but Nature's o'er us!

I saw you blush, you felt me tremble,
In vain would formal art dissemble
All that we wished and thought;
'Twas more than tongue could dare reveal,
'Twas more than virtue ought to feel,
But all that passion ought!

I stooped to cull, with faltering hand,
A shell that, on the golden sand,
Before us faintly gleamed;
I raised it to your lips of dew,
You kissed the shell, I kissed it too—
Good Heaven! how sweet it seemed!

Oh! trust me, 'twas a place, an hour,
The worst that e'er temptation's power
Could tangle me or you in!
Sweet Nea, let us roam no more
Along that wild and lonely shore,
Such walks will be our ruin!

FRANCIS LEDWIDGE

Spring Love

I saw her coming through the flowery grass,
Round her swift ankles butterfly and bee
Blent loud and silent ways; I saw her pass
Where foam-bows shivered on the sunny sea.

Then came the swallow crowding up the dawn.
And cuckoo-echoes filled the dewy south.
I left my love upon the hill, alone,
My last kiss burning on her lovely mouth.

JOHN MONTAGUE

Refrain

I sit in autumn sunlight
on a hotel terrace as I did

when our marriage had begun,
our public honeymoon,

try to unsnarl what went wrong
shouldering all the blame

but no chivalric mode
courtesy's silent discipline

softens the pain
when something is ending

and the tearing begins:
'we shall never be

what we were, again.'
Old love's refrain.

WILLIAM CONGREVE

Song

I tell thee, Charmion, could I time retrieve,
And could again begin to love and live,
To you I should my earliest offering give;
I know my eyes would lead my heart to you,
And I should all my vows and oaths renew,
But to be plain, I never would be true.

For by our weak and weary truth, I find,
Love hates to centre in a point assigned,
But runs with joy the circle of the mind.
Then never let us chain what should be free,
But for relief of either sex agree,
Since women love to change, and so do we.

LADY GREGORY

The Day Draws Near

I think the day draws near when I could stay
Within thy presence with no thought of ill—
And having put all earthliness away
Could listen to thy accents and be still,
And feel no sudden throbbing of the heart
No foolish rising of unbidden tears
Seeing thee come and go—and meet or part
Without this waste of gladness and of fears.
Only have patience for a little space.
I am not yet so wise to see unmoved
Another woman put into my place
Or loved as I was for a moment loved
Be not so cruel as to let me see
The love-light in thine eyes if not for me!

MICHEÁL FANNING

Consolation

I wend to the sea—
the great comforter.
Five times have I
travelled to you
with the stories
of *grande passion*,
All won for a while,
then undone.

You bequeathed a necklace
of shell, to wear,
to alleviate the dolour.

I pace on the soft sand
and seaweed, gentle
it is on my hapless body.

You expunge the pain
of my loves
with the blunging waters,
but just for an instant.

Perhaps I should have remained
on the shoreline,
cogent I was
and wanted her
to be as unsubjugated as the wind.
When I left your bay,
later, I agonised
with the sorrow again.

Then I met a man who said
I had to regenerate from nought.
He knew of the disconsolate journey
towards consolation.

W. B. Yeats

The Song of Wandering Aengus

I went out to the hazel wood,
Because a fire was in my head,
And cut and peeled a hazel wand,
And hooked a berry to a thread;
And when white moths were on the wing,
And moth-like stars were flickering out,
I dropped the berry in a stream
And caught a little silver trout.

When I had laid it on the floor
I went to blow the fire aflame,
But something rustled on the floor,
And some one called me by my name:
It had become a glimmering girl
With apple blossom in her hair
Who called me by my name and ran
And faded through the brightening air.

Though I am old with wandering
Through hollow lands and hilly lands,
I will find out where she has gone,
And kiss her lips and take her hands;

And walk among long dappled grass,
And pluck till time and times are done
The silver apples of the moon,
The golden apples of the sun.

Máire Mhac an Tsaoi

No Second Deirdre

From her own Irish poem

'

'I will not pare my nails.'
That woman said
And turned her back on life,
Because of that one day—
With her clay,
I nor my like
Could never kinship claim—
I comb my hair,
Put colour on my mouth.

Anonymous

I Wish My Love Was a Block of Wood

From Tyrone oral tradition

I wish my love was a block of wood
and I a burning coal.
I'd hold him in my warm embrace
And roast his wee arsehole.

Katharine Tynan

I Wonder Why

I wonder why you came to me last night
O my lost dream that with the midnight fled,—
With all that soft pale glory on your head
And your eyes clear with vision of delight?
Your place is with the dead
The clay and the daisies hide you out of sight.

You are grown fair, my dear. Ah far more fair
Than the familiar fairness that I know.
Is it so sweet below the grass and dew
Is it so sweet forgetting old things there,
nay,—all is well with you
And you forgot not who last night were here.

You gave my lips a drink of comforting
Before you left me at the first cock-crow,
With a long look; for you had far to go
Ere all the rosy shifts of dawn took wing
My singing-bird that sweetly used to sing.

Rhoda Coghill

The Young Bride's Dream

I wonder will he still be gentle
When I am fastened safe to his side?
Will he buy grandeur to cover my beauty,
And shelter me like a bird that he'd hide
In a quiet nest, and show me great courtesies,
And make me queen of his body and all that he is?

Or curse me, use me like a chance woman,
A girl that he'd hire at a fair?
Bid me rip my fine gown to a hundred pieces,
Make rags of it then, for the floors and the stair?
I had warning, last night, in a dream without reason or rhyme;
But the words may be true ones: 'Obedience is ice to the wine.'

Sir Samuel Ferguson

Cashel of Munster

AIR: CLÁR BOG DÉIL
From the Irish

I'd wed you without herds, without money, or rich array,
And I'd wed you on a dewy morning at day-dawn grey;
My bitter woe it is, love, that we are not far away
In Cashel town, though the bare deal board were our marriage-bed this day;

Oh, fair maid, remember the green hill side,
Remember how I hunted about the valleys wide;
Time now, has worn me; my locks are turned to grey,
The year is scarce and I am poor, but send me not, love, away!

Oh, deem not my blood is of base strain, my girl,
Oh, deem not my birth was as the birth of the churl;
Marry me, and prove me, and say soon you will,
That noble blood is written on my right side still!

My purse holds no red gold, no coin of the silver white,
No herds are mine to drive through the long twilight!
But the pretty girl that would take me, all bare though I be and lone
Oh, I'd take her with me kindly to the County Tyrone.

Oh, my girl, I can see 'tis in trouble you are,

And, oh, my girl, I see 'tis your people's reproach you bear:

'I am a girl in trouble for his sake with whom I fly,

And, oh, may no other maiden know such reproach as I!'

DESMOND O'GRADY

The Love War

From the Irish

I'll tell you something for
nothing. There's no war
where more have died
than the love war. I'm surprised
I survived. I'll never give in
to any woman and, between
us, I'm the better for it.
I don't intend to change in that.

The men who die for love leave
their women behind alive.
Then they and the rest of us
have the time of our life
at their absent expense.

The fools die.
The wise survive.
Why die and leave
the women to live?

HELEN SELINA BLACKWOOD

The Irish Emigrant

I'm sitting on the stile, Mary,
Where we sat, side by side,
That bright May morning long ago
When first you were my bride.
The corn was springing fresh and green,
The lark sang loud and high,
The red was on your lip, Mary,
The love-light in your eye.

The place is little changed, Mary,
The day is bright as then,
The lark's loud song is in my ear,
The corn is green again;
But I miss the soft clasp of your hand,
Your breath warm on my cheek,
And I still keep list'ning for the words
You never more may speak.

'Tis but a step down yonder lane,
The little Church stands near—
The Church where we were wed, Mary—
I see the spire from here;
But the graveyard lies between, Mary—

My step might break your rest—
Where you, my darling, lie asleep
With your baby on your breast.

I'm very lonely now, Mary—
The poor make no new friends;—
But, oh! they love the better still
The few our Father sends.
And you were all I had, Mary,
My blessing and my pride;
There's nothing left to care for now
Since my poor Mary died.

Yours was the good brave heart, Mary,
That still kept hoping on,
When trust in God had left my soul,
And half my strength was gone.
There was comfort ever on your lip,
And the kind look on your brow.
I bless you, Mary, for that same,
Though you can't hear me now.

I thank you for the patient smile
When your heart was fit to break;
When the hunger pain was gnawing there
You hid it for my sake.
I bless you for the pleasant word
When your heart was sad and sore.

Oh! I'm thankful you are gone, Mary,
Where grief can't reach you more!

I'm bidding you a long farewell,
My Mary—kind and true!
But I'll not forget you, darling,
In the land I'm going to.
They say there's bread and work for all,
And the sun shines always there;
But I'll not forget old Ireland,
Were it fifty times as fair.

And when amid those grand old woods
I sit and shut my eyes,
My heart will travel back again
To where my Mary lies;
I'll think I see the little stile
Where we sat, side by side,—
And the springing corn and bright May morn,
When first you were my bride.

CHARLES WOLFE

To Mary

If I had thought thou couldst have died,
I might not weep for thee;
But I forgot, when by thy side,
That thou couldst mortal be:
It never through my mind had past
The time would e'er be o'er,
And I on thee should look my last,
And thou shouldst smile no more!

And still upon that face I look,
And think 'twill smile again;
And still the thought I will not brook,
That I must look in vain.
But when I speak—thou dost not say
What thou ne'er left'st unsaid;
And now I feel, as well I may,
Sweet Mary, thou art dead!

If thou wouldst stay, e'en as thou art,
All cold and all serene—
I still might press thy silent heart,
And where thy smiles have been.
While e'en thy chill, bleak course I have,

Thou seemest still mine own;
But there—I lay thee in the grave,
And now I am alone.

I do not think, where'er thou art,
Thou hast forgotten me;
And I, perhaps, may soothe this heart
In thinking too of thee:
Yet there was round thee such a dawn
Of light ne'er seen before,
As fancy never could have drawn,
And never can restore!

Pearse Hutchinson

Into Their True Gentleness

For Katherine Kavanagh

If love is the greatest reality,
and I believe it is,
the gentle are more real
than the violent or than
those like me who
hate violence,
long for gentleness,
but never in our own act
achieve true gentleness.
We fall in love with people
We consider gentle,
we love them violently
for their gentleness,
so violently we drive
them to violence,
for our gentleness
is less real
than their breaking patience,
so falsely we accuse
them of being false.

But with any luck,
time half-opens our eyes
to at least a hundredth
part of our absurdity,
and lets them travel back
released from us,
into their true gentleness,
even with us.

F. R. Higgins

The Roving Lover

If my Love came down from the Mourne hills
To the edge of the white-wood lake,
And hid her head on my pillow now
Before the birds awake,
I would string the stars on a blade of grass
And make my Love a crown
And I'd give my soul for a little kiss
To the girl from the County Down.

I have roamed the roads with my paltry songs
And a wattle in my hand,
But her kindly eyes have led me on
Through a gold and honey land;
And the words I've heard from the noblemen
And the dames of Dublin town
Are cold beside the burning words
Of the girl from the County Down.

The Earl of Longford

Forgetfulness

From the Irish

If now you hate me as you say,
Can you forget so soon
How you and I, the world away,
Once lay and watched the moon?

Can you forget the day when cool
Seemed to our love the sun,
The day that we——? But I'm a fool,
Besides, that day is done.

Can you forget you stroked my hair?
Moist palm upon my brow,
Red mouth, soft breast——. You do not care.
All that's forgotten now.

Have you forgotten too, my flower,
How often you would tell
How God ne'er made until that hour
A man you loved so well?

Can you forget your love for me,
Whom now you do detest?
But that's all one, those times are gone.
No doubt 'tis for the best.

If each could learn as well as I
To profit by my pain,
There's ne'er a man beneath the sky
Would ever love again.

ELEANOR HULL

The Flower of Nut-Brown Maids

From the seventeenth century Irish

If thou wilt come with me to the County of Leitrim,
Flower of Nut-brown Maids—
Honey of bees and mead to the beaker's brim
I'll offer thee, Nut-brown Maid.
Where the pure air floats o'er the swinging boats of the strand,
Under the white-topped wave that laves the edge of the sand,
There without fear we will wander together, hand clasped in hand,
Flower of Nut-brown Maids.

My heart never gave you liking or love,
Said the Flower of Nut-brown Maids;
Though sweet are your words, there's black famine above,
Said the Flower of Nut-brown Maids;
Will gentle words feed me when need and grim hunger come by?
Better be free than with thee to the woodlands to fly;
What gain to us both if together we famish and die?
Wept the Flower of Nut-brown Maids.

I saw her coming towards me o'er the face of the mountain
Like a star glimmering through the mist;
In the field of furze where the slow cows were browsing

In pledge of our love we kissed;
In the bend of the hedge where the tall trees play with the sun,
I wrote her the lines that should bind us for ever in one;
Had you a right to deny me the dues I had won,
O Flower of Nut-brown Maids?

My grief and my torment that thou art not here with me now,
Flower of Nut-brown Maids!
Alone, all alone, it matters not where or how,
O Flower of Nut-brown Maids;
On a slender bed; O little black head, strained close to thee,
Or a heap of hay, until break of day, it were one to me,
Laughing in gladness and glee together, with none to see,
My Flower of Nut-brown Maids.

Thomas Kinsella

Yourself and Myself

From the Irish

If you come at all
come only at night
and walk quietly
—don't frighten me.
You'll find the key
under the doorstep
and me by myself
—don't frighten me.

There's no pot in the way
no stool or can
or rope of straw
—nothing at all.
The dog is quiet
and won't say a word.
It's no shame to him:
I've trained him well.

My mammy's asleep
and my daddy is coaxing her
kissing her mouth

and kissing her mouth.
Isn't she lucky!
Have pity on me
lying here by myself
in the feather bed.

MICHAEL O'SIADHAIL

Welcome

In early spring talk still young and highflown
we laughed, there was an endless time to flirt
and toy with a fable of a year. A snowdrop afloat
in an old wine glass on our table, already grown
tumid with water, lifted the panels of her skirt
to show the pale green hem of her petticoat.

Soon we're strolling along the edge of a bay
kicking over the traces of an early swimmer.
It's deep into June: summer lush and unplanned
rocks us in its lazy arms. In the blaze of day
we paddle in the shallows. I watch in a shimmer
of water the sun doodling honeycombs in the sand.

A year tilts into autumn; after its madcap
race our Russian vine issues its manifesto,
a spray of flower. The sun sloping in humility
smiles its frail approval as old men wrap
against the chill. At last I think I know
half of what we love is love's fragility.

A winter evening as I turn into our street
I hurry to see the rim of light that fingers

around the curtain's edge to tell you're home.
You open the door and I sense as we meet
our moment's wonder. A scent lingers.
I breathe deeply to feed my memory's honeycomb.

George Darley

It Is Not Beauty I Demand

It is not Beauty I demand,
A crystal brow, the moon's despair,
Nor the snow's daughter, a white hand
Nor mermaid's yellow pride of hair.

Tell me not of your starry eyes,
Your lips that seem on roses fed,
Your breasts where Cupid trembling lies
Nor sleeps for kissing of his bed.

A bloomy pair of vermeil cheeks.
Like Hebe's in her ruddiest hours,
A breath that softer music speaks
Than summer winds a-wooing flowers.

These are but gauds; nay, what are lips?
Coral beneath the ocean-stream,
Whose brink when your adventurer sips
Full oft he perishes on them.

And what are cheeks but ensigns oft
That wave hot youth to fields of blood?

Did Helen's breast though ne'er so soft,
Do Greece or Ilium any good?

Eyes can with baleful ardor burn,
Poison can breath that erst perfumed,
There's many a white hand holds an urn
With lovers' hearts to dust consumed.

For crystal brows—there's naught within,
They are but empty cells for pride;
He who the Syren's hair would win
Is mostly strangled in the tide.

Give me, instead of beauty's bust,
A tender heart, a loyal mind,
Which with temptation I could trust,
Yet never linked with error find.

One in whose gentle bosom I
Could pour my secret heart of woes,
Like the care-burdened honey-fly
That hides his murmurs in the rose.

My earthly comforter! whose love
So indefeasible might be,
That when my spirit won above
Hers could not stay for sympathy.

CHRISTY BROWN

What Her Absence Means

It means
no madcap delight will intrude
into the calm flow of my working hours
no ecstatic errors perplex
my literary pretensions.

It means
there will be time enough for thought
undistracted by brown peril of eye
and measured litany of routine deeds
undone by the ghost of a scent.

It means
my neglect of the Sonnets will cease
and Homer come into battle once more.
I might even find turgid old Tennyson
less of a dead loss now.

It means
there will be whole days to spare
for things important to a man—
like learning to live without a woman
without altogether losing one's mind.

It means
there is no one now to read my latest poem
with veiled unhurried eyes
putting my nerves on the feline rack
in silence sheer she-devil hell for me.

It means
there is no silly woman to tell me
'Take it easy—life's long anyway—
don't drink too much—get plenty of sleep—'
and other tremendous clichés.

It means
I am less interrupted now with love.

Brendan Kennelly

The Scarf

It strayed about her head and neck like a
Rumour of something she had never done
Because, the moment ripe, she had no mind to
Yet might have done often, had she chosen.
Where in God's name, I wondered, does it begin
And where on earth may I imagine its end?
Indolent headlands smiled at me, labyrinthine
Rivers flowing into each other wound
And wound about her like desires to praise
Every movement that her body made.
As she moved, so did headlands, rivers too,
Shifting with her as the winter sun laid
Emphasis on colours rumoured in its rays,
Grey-flecked lines of white, delirium of blue.

James Harpur

The Young Man of Galway's Lament

'As Mr Yeats puts it, the countryman's "dream has never been entangled by reality".'
—Lady Gregory, *Poets and Dreamers*, 1901

It was the first week of the falling year.
Your lips had touched the berries of the hedgerows
Leading from my home to the folded hills beyond;
The birds remembered the melodies
Your mouth would sweeten between reflective smiles;
Your absent breathing piled leaves against the wall
And raised the flames higher in the hearth.

You said once that before you would ever leave me
The Slievebloom Mountains would be worn away by wind
The Golden Vale of Tipperary would become as the Syrian desert
The sails of the Norseman would again unfurl the horizon
And snakes would dance a jig on Croagh Patrick's peak.

Your words deceived me, your eyes deepened my belief.
Your dimples were snares I fell headlong into
The pureness of your skin blinded me like snow
Your slender nape prolonged my innocence
And your kisses stole away the days of the week.

Winter brought you back to me.
Your sighs the north wind sent below my door
The stars shivered like the nerve tips of my spine
When the frosted gate-latch clinked and your footfall
Closed in on the top of my neck.
Every night the linen bedsheets tried to recall
The lolling heat and fragrance of your limbs.

You told me once I was the king of Munster,
The king of Ulster, the king of Connacht,
The king of Leinster, the high king of Tara,
And that one thought of malice towards you
Would summon the feral armies of the Danes
The chain-mailed horses of the Norman knights
And the cold stare of the English men-at-arms.

The round towers of Ireland lie in ruin
Homesteads feed their stones to all the walls around them
The hermits have departed from the hills
The crows pick entrails from the broken roads
The rains boil the fields to slurry
But there never once took root in my breast
A single dark thought about you.

You played the goose with me, you dallied with me,
You said the young men of Clare and Galway
At night when they lay with their women
All gazed on your face, your parted lips.

Your hair you said flashed the fire of a conquistador,
Your cheekbones were fashioned in Córdoba,
Your ankles were as fine as those of Queen Isabella.

When spring came it brought the memory of the spring before,
The morning we opened every door and window
And all the vapours smoking from the boglands
And all the vapours thinning down from clouds
Had suddenly vanished like Agamemnon's fleet at Troy
And the colours of the hills and meadows were restored
In the gentle thaw of softened air.
There was rejoicing in the land
As if all the fiddle players from Cork to Donegal
Had opened their windows to let their stringy music
Rise over trees and onward into river valleys
Over loughs and mountains into the breasts
Of every man, woman and child.

Summer will soon come upon the land.
It was the time you took yourself away
The time when wheat spilled over from the fields
The copper beeches flounced their heavy dresses
And the early sun blanched the stones of hilltop cairns.
Do you now dine at the table of a gentleman
And avert your eyes into a silver cup of wine?
Did you fall in with the tinkers of Leitrim or Fermanagh?
Or did you cross the ocean to the western isles
Where the salmon leap and the hazelnuts abound?

I will tell the sparrows to look for your blue dress
The winds will blow to me your spoor
The rivers will pass along your reflections
Churches will sound their bells if you should cross their thresholds:
At night the owls will spy the tracks and pathways
And the eyes of fish will break the surfaces of lakes.

You will hear my thoughts when I think of you at night.
When I read, your eyes will trace each word with mine
I will walk beside you as you walk
And rise with you from your bed.
I am before you, I am behind you,
I am above you, I am below you,
I am the rain that softens the ground you tread,

The wind that parts the hair from your face
The sun that settles like a halo on your shoulders
And the moon that dims your shadow
Wherever, like a shade, you flit, soundless
Over fairy mounds, through ancient woods,
Beside the streams that gush from wounded mountains,
Over bridges, past holy wells and crossroads,
Through the height, width and depth of Ireland.

Thomas Kinsella

Lay Your Weapons Down, Young Lady

From the Irish of Pierás Feiriteár

Lay your weapons down, young lady.
Do you want to ruin us all?
Lay your weapons down, or else
I'll have you under royal restraint.

These weapons put behind you:
hide henceforth your curling hair;
do not bare that white breast
that spares no living man.

Lady, do you believe
you've never killed, to North or South?
Your mild eye-glance has killed at large
without the need of knife or axe.

You may think your knee's not sharp
and think your palm is soft:
to wound a man, believe me,
you need no knife or spear!

Hide your lime-white bosom,
show not your tender flank.
For love of Christ let no one see
your gleaming breast, a tuft in bloom.

Conceal those eyes of grey
if you'd go free for all you've killed.
Close your lips, to save your soul;
let your bright teeth not be seen.

Not few you have done to death:
do you think you're not mortal clay?
In justice, put your weapons down
and let us have no further ruin.

If you've terrified all you want,
lady who seek my downfall,
now—before I am sunk in soil—
your weapons, lay them down.

What your surname is, young lady,
I leave to puzzle the world.
But add an 'a' or an 'e'
and it gives your Christian name away.

Jonathan Swift

Holyhead. September 25, 1727

Lo here I sit at Holyhead
With muddy ale and mouldy bread:
All Christian victuals stink of fish,
I'm where my enemies would wish.
Convict of lies is every sign,
The inn has not one drop of wine.
I'm fastened both by wind and tide,
I see the ship at anchor ride.
The captain swears the sea's too rough,
He has not passengers enough.
And thus the Dean is forced to stay,
Till others come to help the pay.
In Dublin they'd be glad to see
A packet though it brings in me.
They cannot say the winds are cross;
Your politicians at a loss
For want of matter swears and frets,
Are forced to read the old gazettes.
I never was in haste before
To reach that slavish hateful shore:
Before, I always found the wind
To me was most malicious kind,
But now the danger of a friend

On whom my hopes and fears depend,
Absent from whom all climes are cursed,
With whom I'm happy in the worst,
With rage impatient makes me wait
A passage to the land I hate.
Else, rather on this bleaky shore
Where loudest winds incessant roar,
Where neither herb nor tree will thrive,
Where nature hardly seems alive,
I'd go in freedom to my grave,
Than rule yon isle and be a slave.

Thomas Moore

Love Thee, Dearest? Love Thee?

Love thee, dearest? love thee?
Yes, by yonder star I swear,
Which through tears above thee
Shines so sadly fair;
Though often dim
With tears, like him,
Like him my truth will shine,
And—love thee, dearest? love thee?
Yes, till death I'm thine.

Leave thee, dearest? leave thee?
No, that star is not more true;
When my vows deceive thee,
He will wander too.
Adored of night
My veil his light,
And death shall darken mine
But—leave thee, dearest? Leave thee?
No, till Death I'm thine.

John Boyle O'Reilly

Love Was True to Me

Love was true to me,
True and tender;
I who ought to be
Love's defender,
Let the cold winds blow
Till they chilled him;
Let the winds and snow
Shroud him—and I know
That I killed him.

Years he cried to me
To be kinder;
I was blind to see
And grew blinder.
Years with soft hands raised
Fondly reaching,
Wept and prayed and praised,
Still beseeching.

When he died I woke,
God! how lonely,
When the grey dawn broke
On one only.

Now beside Love's grave
I am kneeling;
All he sought and gave
I am feeling.

BLANAID SALKELD

That Corner

Man is most anxious not to stir
Out of the unblessed beat
Of sounds that recur
In house or on street.
Not only the birds' morning prayers,
But light steppings up stairs,
Rap on the bedroom door,
·We have heart-beats for.
The postman's knock, though it spill
Rejection and vulgar bill—
At noon, the baker's basket creaks;
Hooves, hoots, factory-shrieks;
Hollow tattle of the trams;
Or a door slams;
Buzz of flies; chapel bells,
And a thousand sounds else.
The casual spirit poises,
Elegantly,
Tired of being free,
Between the usual noises.
Love's mood, however,
Is contrary to this hankering,
This holding on to the seat

Of life's speeding jolty car.
Love is in a fever
To escape the tinkering
Minutes that beat—
Familiar,
Only varied by fear—
On eye and ear.
Now I would leap clear.
What bait shall I procure to lure him out of time?
Not from the sea into the salty drought—
But cleanly out
Of days' and nights' faint metre and false rhyme,
To hold him safe
Round final angle,
Corner, where no jangle-tangle
Makes stir to chafe:
From this inadequate night and day,
I would steal him away.

J. M. SYNGE

A Wish

May one sorrow every day
Your festivity waylay.
May seven tears in every week
From your well of pleasure leak
That I—signed with such a dew—
May for my full pittance sue
Of the Love forever curled
Round the maypole of the world.

Heavy riddles lie in this,
Sorrow's sauce for every kiss.

DESMOND O'GRADY

In the Greenwood

From the Irish

I

My darling, my love,
Together let's rove
Through the forest so flagrantly scenting.
By trout streams we'll rest,
Watch the thrush build her nest,
While the doe and the roe buck are calling.
Each ring singing bird
In the wild wind wood heard
And the cuckoo high up in the plane trees
And never will come
Death into our home
In the shade of the sweet scented green-trees.

II

O beautiful head
All kiss curled red,
Green and grand your eyes are.
My heart is high-strung,
Like a thread too well spun.
From loving too long from afar.

Frank O'Connor

The Body's Speech

From the Irish of Donal MacCarthy More, Earl Clancarthy

My grief, my grief, maid without sin,
Mother of God's Son,
Because of one I cannot win
My peace is gone.

Mortal love, a raging flood,
O Mother Maid,
Runs like a fever through my blood,
Ruins heart and head.

How can I tell her of my fear,
My wild desire,
When words I speak for my own ear
Turn me to fire?

I dream of breasts so lilylike,
Without a fleck,
And hair that, bundled up from her back,
Burdens her neck.

And praise the cheeks where flames arise
That shame the rose,

And the soft hands at whose touch flees
All my repose.

Since I have seen her I am lost,
A man possessed,
Better to feel the world gone past,
Earth on my breast;

And from my tomb to hear the choir,
The hum of prayer;
Without her while her place is here,
My peace is there.

I am a ghost upon your path,
A wasting death,
But you must know one word of truth
Gives a ghost breath—

In language beyond learning's touch
Passion can teach—
Speak in that speech beyond reproach
The body's speech.

Douglas Hyde

My Grief on the Sea

From the Irish

My grief on the sea,
How the waves of it roll!
For they heave between me
And the love of my soul!

Abandoned, forsaken,
To grief and to care,
Will the sea ever waken
Relief from despair?

My grief, and my trouble!
Would he and I were
In the Province of Leinster,
Or County of Clare.

Were I and my darling—
Oh, heart-bitter wound!—
On board of the ship
For America bound.

On a green bed of rushes
All last night I lay,
And I flung it abroad
With the heat of the day.

And my love came behind me—
He came from the south;
His breast to my bosom,
His mouth to my mouth.

Michael Hartnett

Quicksand

From the Irish of Nuala Ní Dhomhnaill

My love, don't let me, going to sleep
fall into the dark cave.
I fear the sucking sand
I fear the eager hollows in the water,
places with bogholes underground.
Down there there's ancient wood and bogdeal
the Fianna's bones are there at rest
With rustless swords—and a drowned girl,
a noose around her neck.

Now there is an ebb-tide:
the moon is full, the sea will leave the land
and tonight when I close my eyes
let there be terra firma, let there be hard sand.

Padraic Colum

She Moved Through the Fair

My young love said to me, 'My brothers won't mind,
And my parents won't slight you for your lack of kind.'
Then she stepped away from me, and this she did say
'It will not be long, love, till our wedding day.'

She stepped away from me and she moved through the fair.
And fondly I watched her go here and go there,
Then she went her way homeward with one star awake,
As the swan in the evening moves over the lake.

The people were saying no two were e'er wed
But one had a sorrow that never was said,
And I smiled as she passed with her goods and her gear,
And that was the last that I saw of my dear.

I dreamt it last night that my young love came in,
So softly she entered, her feet made no din;
She came close beside me, and this she did say
'It will not be long, love, till our wedding day.'

GABRIEL FITZMAURICE

In the Midst of Possibility

Now I love you
Free of me:
In this loving I can see
The YOU of you
Apart from me—
The YOU of you that's ever free.

This is the YOU I love.
This is the YOU I'll never have:
This is the YOU beyond possession—
The YOU that's ever true
While ever changing,
Ever new.

Now,
Naked
Free,
The YOU of you
Meets the ME of me
And to see is to love;
To love, to see:

In the midst of possibility
We agree.

LADY GREGORY

Donall Oge: Grief of a Girl's Heart

From the Irish

O Donall Oge, if you go across the sea,
Bring myself with you and do not forget it;
And you will have a sweetheart for fair days and market days,
And the daughter of the King of Greece beside you at night.

It is late last night the dog was speaking of you;
The snipe was speaking of you in her deep marsh.
It is you are the lonely bird through the woods;
And that you may be without a mate until you find me.

You promised me, and you said a lie to me,
That you would be before me where the sheep are flocked;
I gave a whistle and three hundred cries to you,
And I found nothing there but a bleating lamb.

You promised me a thing that was hard for you,
A ship of gold under a silver mast;
Twelve towns with a market in all of them,
And a fine white court by the side of the sea.

You promised me a thing that is not possible,
That you would give me gloves of the skin of a fish;

That you would give me shoes of the skin of a bird;
And a suit of the dearest silk in Ireland.

O Donall Oge, it is I would be better to you
Than a high, proud, spendthrift lady:
I would milk the cow; I would bring help to you;
And if you were hard pressed, I would strike a blow for you.

O, ochone, and it's not with hunger
Or with wanting food, or drink, or sleep,
That I am growing thin, and my life is shortened;
But it is the love of a young man has withered me away.

It is early in the morning that I saw him coming,
Going along the road on the back of a horse;
He did not come to me; he made nothing of me;
And it is on my way home that I cried my fill.

When I go by myself to the Well of Loneliness,
I sit down and I go through my trouble;
When I see the world and do not see my boy,
He that has an amber shade in his hair.

It was on that Sunday I gave my love to you;
The Sunday that is last before Easter Sunday.
And myself on my knees reading the Passion;
And my two eyes giving love to you for ever.

O, aya! my mother, give myself to him;
And give him all that you have in the world;
Get out yourself to ask for alms,
And do not come back and forward looking for me.

My mother said to me not to be talking with you to-day,
Or tomorrow, or on Sunday;
It was a bad time she took for telling me that;
It was shutting the door after the house was robbed.

My heart is as black as the blackness of the sloe,
Or as the black coal that is on the smith's forge;
Or as the sole of a shoe left in white halls;
It was you put that darkness over my life.

You have taken the east from me; You have taken the west from me,
You have taken what is before me and what is behind me;
You have taken the moon, you have taken the sun from me,
And my fear is great that you have taken God from me!

Jeremiah Joseph Callanan

The Outlaw of Loch Lene

O many a day have I made good ale in the glen,
That came not of stream, or malt, like the brewing of men.
My bed was the ground, my roof, the greenwood above,
And the wealth that I sought—one far kind glance from my love.

Alas! on that night when the horses I drove from the field,
That I was not near from terror my angel to shield.
She stretched forth her arms,—her mantle she flung to the wind,
And swam o'er Loch Lene, her outlawed lover to find.

O would that a freezing sleet-winged tempest did sweep,
And I and my love were alone far off on the deep!
I'd ask not a ship, or a bark, or pinnace to save,—
With her hand round my waist, I'd fear not the wind or the wave.

'Tis down by the lake where the wild tree fringes its sides,
The maid of my heart, the fair one of Heaven resides—
I think as at eve she wanders its mazes along,
The birds go to sleep by the sweet wild twist of her song.

Patrick MacDonogh

She Walked Unaware

O, she walked unaware of her own increasing beauty
That was holding men's thoughts from market or plough,
As she passed by, intent on her womanly duties,
And she without leisure to be wayward or proud;
Or if she had pride then it was not in her thinking
But thoughtless in her body like a flower of good breeding.
The first time I saw her spreading coloured linen
Beyond the green willow she gave me gentle greeting
With no more intention than the leaning willow tree.

Though she smiled without intention yet from that day forward
Her beauty filled like water the four corners of my being,
And she rested in my heart like the hare in the form
That is shaped to herself. And I that would be singing
Or whistling at all times went silently then;
Till I drew her aside among straight stems of beeches
When the blackbird was sleeping and promised that never
The fields would be ripe but I'd gather all sweetness,
A red moon of August would rise on our wedding.

October is spreading bright flame along stripped willows
Low fires of the dogwood burn down to grey water,—
God pity me now and all desolate sinners

Demented with beauty! I have blackened my thought
In drouths of bad longing, and all brightness goes shrouded
Since he came with his rapture of wild words that mirrored
Her beauty and made her ungentle and proud.
Tonight she will spread her brown hair on his pillow
But I shall be hearing the harsh cries of wild fowl.

Richard Weber

Lady and Gentleman

Of himself to think this: she does not
Know my meaning nor ever will,
Though the leaves like late butterflies
Twist and turn, falter and fall
In the outside racing, interlacing winds.

And she, seeing this, that and that
Other yet sees nothing of these,
Is contemplative in her conducted contempt
Of this contact of the customary, this always
And always to be expected, the look of love.

And all else but herself: herself she sees
And is pleased and displeased by turns
Of her thought, of her head also.
One can see it in the constant,
Constrained movements of her denying head.

So fine a thing this is, balanced like held
Breath between beauty and plainness.
When the eyes hold one, they hold so fast
It is only by one's arrival at their awaiting
Uninterest that one releases, is released, dropped.

To fall as one can in one's napkin,
Like a soupdrop, desiring not to be noticed.
Nevertheless, nerveless, one looks up to see
If she can see. Then what joy that she sees,
What, you? No, she watches not you, not

Even now the appearance of you. What, then?
He has seen already that in that steady
Amazing gaze of her eyes there is merely
Awareness of self, herself, and maybe not
Only that, but of whole hordes of women

Who have come together in this one woman.
It is not enough, he knows, but it is more
Than one man, representing only himself,
Can bear, which is why shortly he must dab
At his dismayed mouth with his already raised napkin.

Kuno Meyer

Liadan and Curithir

From the Irish

CURITHIR
Of late
Since I parted from Liadin,
Long as a month is every day,
Long as a year each month.

LIADIN
Joyless
The bargain I have made!
The heart of him I loved I wrung.

'Twas madness
Not to do his pleasure,
Were there not the fear of Heaven's King.

'Twas a trifle
That wrung Curithir's heart against me:
To him great was my gentleness.

A short while I was
In the company of Curithir:
Sweet was my intimacy with him.

The music of the forest
Would sing to me when with Curithir,
Together with the voice of the purple sea.

Would that
Nothing of all I have done
Should have wrung his heart against me!

Conceal it not!
He was my heart's love,
Whatever else I might love.

A roaring flame
Has dissolved this heart of mine—
Without him for certain it cannot live.

W. E. H. LECKY

The Decline of Love

Oh, broken-hearted lover,
Who touched us long ago,
The days seem well-nigh over
When tears like yours can flow.

Great poets still rise, bringing
Thoughts subtle, deep and strong;
But scarcely one is singing
A simple lover's song.

A graver age uncloses
Which mocks at Cupid's barb,
And Venus hides her roses
In Academic garb.

Ambition, science, learning,
And countless efforts more,
And many lamps are burning
But very few to Love.

Thought strengthens more than feeling,
And each takes wider range;
And most wounds find their healing
In lines of ceaseless change

And to the young man's vision
New star-like spheres unfold,
Which promise fields Elysian,
Quite other than of old.

And so the world advances,
And none can bid it stay;
Yet still the heart romances,
Although the head be grey.

And in stray dreams of passion
The old days sometimes rise,
When Love was still the fashion;
Before the world grew wise.

JAMES EYRE WEEKES

Poem Left in a Lady's Toilet

Oh that I was my Sylvia's stays!
to clasp her lovely waist,
to press those breasts, where rapture plays,
where love and pleasure feast.

That I was but her smock so white,
to feel her velvet skin,
to bless my touch with soft delight
and kiss it without sin.

Or that I was her stocking neat,
gartered above her knee,
that I, so near the happy seat,
the happy seat might see.

Why am I not her lace, her ring,
her dicky or her fan,
her dog, her monkey, anything
but what I am—a man.

Answer by the Lady's Maid

Ah simple poet, ill-judged prayer!
how like an owl you sing,
better for thee the ring to wear
than be thyself the ring.

Where is thy feeling, senseless stock?
thou injudicious Elf—
better for thee to lift the smock
than be the smock itself.

Would you, fond simpleton, desire
to be your lady's fan,
If you would nightly cool her fire
Wish still to be a man.

S. Charles Jellicoe

Advice to a Lover

Oh! if you love her,
Show her the best of you;
So will you move her
To bear with the rest of you.
Coldness and jealousy
Cannot but seem to her
Signs that a tempest lurks
Where was sunbeam to her.
Patience and tenderness
Still will awake in her
Hopes of new sunshine,
Tho' the storm break for her;
Love, she will know, for her,
Like the blue firmament,
Under the tempest lies
Gentle and permanent.
Nor will she ever
Gentleness find the less,
When the storm overblown
Leaveth clear kindliness.
Deal with her tenderly,
Skylike above her,
Smile on her waywardness,
Oh! if you love her.

Leonard Macnally

The Lass of Richmond Hill

On Richmond hill there lives a lass
More bright than May day morn,
Whose charms all other maids surpass
A rose without a thorn.
This lass so neat with smiles so sweet
Has won my right good will,
I'd crowns resign to call her mine,
Sweet lass of Richmond hill,
Sweet lass of Richmond hill,
Sweet lass of Richmond hill.
I'd crowns resign to call her mine,
Sweet lass of Richmond hill.

Ye zephyrs gay that fan the air
And wanton through the grove
Oh! whisper to my charming fair
'I die for her and love'
This lass so neat with smiles so sweet
Has won my right good will,
I'd crowns resign to call her mine,
Sweet lass of Richmond hill,
Sweet lass of Richmond hill,

Sweet lass of Richmond hill.
I'd crowns resign to call her mine,
Sweet lass of Richmond hill.

How happy will the shepherd be
Who calls this nymph his own.
Oh! may her choice be fixed on me,
Mine's fixed on her alone.
This lass so neat with smiles so sweet
Has won my right good will,
I'd crowns resign to call her mine,
Sweet lass of Richmond hill,
Sweet lass of Richmond hill,
Sweet lass of Richmond hill.
I'd crowns resign to call her mine,
Sweet lass of Richmond hill.

W. B. Yeats

The Folly of Being Comforted

One that is ever kind said yesterday:
'Your well-belovèd's hair has threads of grey,
And little shadows come about her eyes;
Time can but make it easier to be wise
Though now it seems impossible, and so
All that you need is patience.'

Heart cries, 'No,
I have not a crumb of comfort, not a grain.
Time can but make her beauty over again:
Because of that great nobleness of hers
The fire that stirs about her, when she stirs,
Burns but more clearly. O she had not these ways
When all the wild summer was in her gaze.

O heart! O heart! if she'd but turn her head,
You'd know the folly of being comforted.

MAEVE KELLY

Half Century

Others have not been lucky as we
Who have shared these generous times,
Welding together even in absence
Every present moment, so that we become
Almost one flesh, each self-sufficient
Though interdependent. Siamese twins.
It would not be true to say there have been
No rows, no flurry of disparate views,
Flaring to rooftop high
Our loud sundering of old vows.
They have been rare and only memorable
Because of that.
Yet our lives have not been placid—
The usual deaths, the common griefs,
The surge and swell of children,
Bad school reports, drugs in a window box,
Even the policeman at the door.

When I look back through my half century
I am astonished to discover
That for only half of it
I have known you. The other half
Collapses on itself by this default.

That first growth seems in retrospect
A kind of vagrancy, a maverick uncertainty
Without anchorage. An unrewarded search.

I am overwhelmed by the dicey chance of this.
Other lovers write in praise
Or in cherished recall of the intimacies
Which, being secret, are shattered by a phrase.
I cannot describe the puzzle we have made,
Jig-sawing miraculously, fitting our variety,
Our patchwork lives, our woven cloth,
Many-textured, many-coloured, into this tent
With which we clothe and house ourselves.

These are the things we have together made,
Gardens and houses, walls I know will stand
Long after we are gone. Vistas have opened
And closed to our command,
And the buttressed land has been breached
, And yielded a little. All may remain
When we unfold ourselves in twin plots
And return separately to that dust
Which gave us common sustenance. It is a grief
I dare not ponder, our separate deaths.
Will we, I wonder, for the next half
Of half a century, with unexplored insight
Unwind, unfold, untangle twined-over roots from roots,

Unravel time itself so that we may slide
Placidly back to birth, and finally divide?

All those unsayable words
You, being private, regard as sacred
Will have found their place.
Can these things we have made
Speak of them, our loves, our fears, our griefs?
Or the nonsensical breakfast discussions,
Politics, the day's bombings, the brute maimings,
The tattered fabric of our outer lives?
Is that what we will leave?

Lovers who are permitted
Mirrored glimpses of each other
Forget the privilege and become familiar.
We have somehow escaped such despair,
Are constantly amused by the absurd.
Perhaps we share
A half-witted simpleness
And regard the world
Through the other's innocence.

RICHARD KELL

Spring Night

For Muriel

Out on Killiney Hill that night, you said
'Remember how we promised to come up here
When snow is lying under a full moon?'
And I made no reply—to hide my sadness,
Thinking we might not satisfy that whim,
Ever perhaps, at least for years to come,
Since it was spring, and winter would see us parted.

Sitting on the Druid's Chair recalled
The last time we were there, a night of icy
Wind and moonlight when the sea was churning
Silver and the distant hills were clear;
How we belonged to them and they to us.
Now there was no brightness—only a vast
Obscurity confusing sea and sky,
Dalkey Island and the lights of Bray
Submerged and suffocating in the mist.

And there was no belonging now; no vivid
Elemental statement to compel
Refusal or assent, making decision

Easy; but a dumb neutrality
That challenged us to give it character
And view our own minds large as a landscape.
To you it was tranquil. Sinister to me.

Lying under the pine tree, looking up
At the small stars and breathing the wood's sweetness,
We spoke hardly a word. I could not tell you
I was afraid of something out there
In the future, like that dark and bitter sea;
And how my love for you would have me lonely
Until the fear was broken. I could say
'Be close to me this winter and every winter;
We'll come up here to watch the snow by moonlight'—
And that would be too easy. For I must give
To you whose meaning transcends moods and moments
Nothing half-hearted or ambiguous,
But the perfected diamond of my will.

W. B. YEATS

The Lover Mourns for the Loss of Love

Pale brows, still hands and dim hair,
I had a beautiful friend
And dreamed that the old despair
Would end in love in the end:
She looked in my heart one day
And saw your image was there;
She has gone weeping away.

Austin Clarke

The Envy of Poor Lovers

Pity poor lovers who may not do what they please
With their kisses under a hedge, before a raindrop
Unhouses it; and astir from wretched centuries,
Bramble and briar remind them of the saints.

Her envy is the curtain seen at night-time,
Happy position that could change her name.
His envy—clasp of the married whose thoughts can be alike,
Whose nature flows without the blame or shame.

Lying in the grass as if it were a sin
To move, they hold each other's breath, tremble,
Ready to share that ancient dread—kisses begin
Again—of Ireland keeping company with them.

Think, children, of institutions mured above
Your ignorance, where every look is veiled,
State-paid to snatch away the folly of poor lovers
For whom, it seems, the sacraments have failed.

FERGUS ALLEN

A Time for Blushing

For Joan

Plain-clothes inspectors are operating in this store,
In this station and these offices, on every floor.

Dog is reportedly eating dog at the street corners
And television crews focus on the griefs of mourners,

But the inspectors are using listening devices
To harken to the angels calling the starting prices.

Like lymph, they lead shadowy lives, keeping out of sight,
And, like phagocytes, they are always in the right.

Sometimes we may spot them in alcoves, transmitting orders
Or murmuring into miniature tape recorders.

From attics above the bankers' plaza and its fountains,
Encrypted reports go to antennae on the mountains.

They move amongst us unnoticed, in lovat and fawn,
Catching us when we order a drink or mow the lawn.

From lairs in mock orange and dogwood, spectacled eyes
Interpret my movements, read my lips and note my lies,

And remotely controlled bees employ their working hours
Dictating my sins into the corollas of flowers.

The poplars flap their tongues on the far side of the wall,
And the plain-clothes inspectorate overhears it all.

So it's silence for us, my love, it's silence in bed—
And what I was about to say had better not be said.

Anonymous

To the Lady with a Book

Translated from the thirteenth- to seventeenth-century Irish by Frank O'Connor

Pleasant journey, little book
To that gay gold foolish head!
Though I wish that you remained
And I travelled in your stead.

Gentle book, 'tis well for you,
Hastening where my darling rests;
You will see the crimson lips,
You will touch the throbbing breasts.

You will see the dear grey eye.
On you will that hand alight—
Ah, my grief 'tis you not I
Will rest beside her warm at night.

You will see the slender brows
And the white nape's candle-gleam,
And the fond flickering cheeks of youth
That I saw last night in dream.

And the waist my arms would clasp
And the long legs and stately feet
That pace between my sleep and me
With their magic you will meet.

And the soft pensive sleepy voice
Whose echoes murmur in my brain
Will bring you rest—'tis well for you!
When shall I hear that voice again?

Michael Longley

The Linen Industry

Pulling up flax after the blue flowers have fallen
And laying our handfuls in the peaty water
To rot those grasses to the bone, or building stooks
That recall the skirts of an invisible dancer,

We become a part of the linen industry
And follow its processes to the grubby town
Where fields are compacted into window-boxes
And there is little room among the big machines.

But even in our attic under the skylight
We make love on a bleach green, the whole meadow
Draped with material turning white in the sun
As though snow reluctant to melt were our attire.

What's passion but a battering of stubborn stalks,
Then a gentle combing out of fibres like hair
And a weaving of these into christening robes,
Into garments for a marriage or funeral?

Since it's like a bereavement once the labour's done
To find ourselves last workers in a dying trade,

Let flax be our matchmaker, our undertaker,
The provider of sheets for whatever the bed—

And be shy of your breasts in the presence of death,
Say that you look more beautiful in linen
Wearing white petticoats, the bow on your bodice
A butterfly attending the embroidered flowers.

W. R. RODGERS

The Net

Quick, woman, in your net
Catch the silver I fling!
O I am deep in your debt,
Draw tight, skin-tight, the string,
And rake the silver in.
No fisher ever yet
Drew such a cunning ring.

Ah, shifty as the fin
Of any fish this flesh
That, shaken to the shin,
Now shoals into your mesh,
Bursting to be held in;
Purse-proud and pebble-hard,
Its pence like shingle showered.

Open the haul, and shake
The fill of shillings free,
Let all the satchels break
And leap about the knee
In shoals of ecstasy.
Guineas and gills will flake
At each gull-plunge of me.

Though all the angels, and
Saint Michael at their head,
Nightly contrive to stand
On guard about your bed,
Yet none dare take a hand,
But each can only spread
His eagle-eye instead.

But I, being man, can kiss
And bed-spread-eagle too;
All flesh shall come to this,
Being less than angel is,
Yet higher far in bliss
As it entwines with you.

Come, make no sound, my sweet;
Turn down the candid lamp
And draw the equal quilt
Over our naked guilt.

Douglas Hyde

Ringleted Youth of My Love

From the Irish

Ringleted youth of my love,
With thy locks bound loosely behind thee,
You passed by the road above,
But you never came in to find me;
Where were the harm for you
If you came for a little to see me,
Your kiss is a wakening dew
Were I ever so ill or so dreamy.

If I had golden store
I would make a nice little boreen,
To lead straight up to his door,
The door of the house of my storeen;
Hoping to God not to miss
The sound of his footfall in it,
I have waited so long for his kiss
That for days I have slept not a minute.

I thought, O my love! you were so—
As the moon is, or sun on a fountain,
And I thought after that you were snow,

The cold snow on top of the mountain;
And I thought after that, you were more
Like God's lamp shining to find me,
Or the bright star of knowledge before,
And the star of knowledge behind me.

You promised me high-heeled shoes,
And satin and silk, my storeen,
And to follow me, never to lose,
Though the ocean were round us roaring
Like a bush in a gap in a wall
I am now left lonely without thee,
And this house I grow dead of, is all
That I see around or about me.

ESTHER JOHNSON ('STELLA')

Stella to Dr Swift

on his birth-day, November 30, 1721

St Patrick's Dean, your country's pride,
My early and my only Guide,
Let me among the rest attend,
Your pupil and your humble friend,
To celebrate in female strains
The day that paid your mother's pains;
Descend to take that tribute due
In gratitude alone to you.

When men began to call me fair,
You interposed your timely care:
You early taught me to despise
The ogling of a coxcomb's eyes;
Showed where my judgment was misplaced;
Refined my fancy and my taste.
Behold that beauty just decayed,
Invoking Art to Nature's aid:
Forsook by her admiring train,
She spreads her tattered nets in vain;
Short was her part upon the stage;
Went smoothly on for half a page;

Her bloom was gone, she wanted Art
As the scene changed, to change her part;
She, whom no lover could resist
Before the second Act was hissed.
Such is the fate of female race
With no endowments but a face;
Before the thirtieth year of life,
A maid forlorn or hated wife.

Stella to you, her tutor, owes
That she has ne'er resembled those;
Nor was a burthen to mankind
With half her course of years behind.
You taught how I might youth prolong
By knowing what was right and wrong;
How from my heart to bring supplies
Of lustre to my fading eyes;
How soon a beauteous mind repairs
The loss of changed or falling hairs;
How wit and virtue from within
Send out a smoothness o'er the skin;
Your lectures could my fancy fix,
And I can please at thirty-six.

The sight of Chloe at fifteen
Coquetting, gives me not the spleen;
The idol now of every fool
Till Time shall make their passions cool;

Then tumbling down Time's steepy hill,
While Stella holds her station still.

O! turn your precepts into laws,
Redeem the women's ruined cause,
Retrieve lost empire to our sex,
That men may bow their rebel necks.
Long be the day that gave you birth
Sacred to friendship, wit and mirth;
Late dying may you cast a shred
Of your rich mantle o'er my head;
To bear with dignity my sorrow,
One day alone, then die tomorrow.

Paul Durcan

Sally

Sally, I was happy with *you*.

Yet a dirty cafeteria in a railway station—
In the hour before dawn over a formica table
Confetti'ed with cigarette ash and coffee stains—
Was all we ever knew of a home together.

'Give me a child and let me go.'
'Give me a child and let me stay.'
She to him and he to her;
Which said *which*? and *who* was *who*?

Sally, I was happy with *you*.

OLIVER GOLDSMITH

The Gift

To Iris, in Bow Street, Covent Garden.
Imitated from the French

Say, cruel Iris, pretty rake,
Dear mercenary beauty,
What annual offering shall I make
Expressive of my duty?

My heart, a victim to thine eyes,
Should I at once deliver,
Say, would the angry fair one prize
The gift, who slights the giver?

A bill, a jewel, watch, or toy,
My rivals give—and let 'em;
If gems, or gold, impart a joy,
I'll give them—when I get 'em.

I'll give—but not the full-blown rose,
Or rose-bud more in fashion:
Such short-lived off'rings but disclose
A transitory passion.

I'll give thee something yet unpaid,
Not less sincere than civil,
I'll give thee—ah! too charming maid!
I'll give thee—to the Devil.

HERBERT TRENCH

She Comes Not When Noon Is on the Roses

She comes not when Noon is on the roses—
Too bright is Day
She comes not to the Soul till it reposes
From work and play

But when Night is on the hills, and the great Voices
Roll in from sea,
By starlight and by candlelight and dreamlight
She comes to me.

MICHAEL LONGLEY

A Touch

From the Irish

She is the touch of pink
On crab apple blossom
And hawthorn, and she melts
Frostflowers with her finger.

OSCAR WILDE

La Dame Jaune

She took the curious amber charms
From off her neck, and laid them down,
She loosed her jonquil-coloured gown,
And shook the bracelets from her arms.

She loosed her lemon-satin stays,
She took a carven ivory comb,
Her hair crawled down like yellow foam,
And flickered in the candle's rays.

I watched her thick locks, like a mass
Of honey, dripping from the pin;
Each separate hair was as the thin
Gold thread within a Venice glass.

BRYAN GUINNESS, LORD MOYNE

The Forlorn Queen

She trod the edge of land
And felt the softness of the desolate sand:
And where the waves began
With pearls her ankles ran.

Bitterly she wished
For the sweet days that were vanished:
From those eyes that his lips had kissed
The salt sea was nourished.

Francis Ledwidge

The Meeting

She'll meet me with the gate thrown wide,
The sunset red upon her grace,
Loud will her heart be in her side
And white the excitement on her face.
And song and wing shall fill the place,
And murmuring of a new moon's tide.

Strange shall her story be, and long,
And old her love as the blue sea.
In her white presence growing strong
Of all my cares I shall be free.
And with her through the years to be
Live where wing-shadows shake with song.

AUGUSTUS YOUNG

She's My Love

From the Irish

She's my love,
who only gives me trouble;
although she has made me ill,
no woman serves me as well.

She's my dear,
who breaks me and doesn't care;
who yawns when I take my leave,
O she won't grieve on my grave.

She's my precious,
with eyes as green as grass is,
who won't touch my bending head,
or take presents for caresses.

She's my secret,
not a word from her I get;
she's deaf to me as the skies,
and never lets our eyes meet.

She's my problem
(strange, how long death takes to come),
this woman won't come near me,
still I swear, she's my loved one.

Theo Dorgan

Up All Night

From the Irish

Since moonrise last evening I'm here like a fool sitting up,
Feeding the fire and poking the embers and coals,
The house is asleep and I'm here on my own all the night,
Here's the cock crowing and everyone snoring but me.

All I can see is your mouth, your brow and your cheek,
Your burning blue eye that robbed me of quiet and peace,
Lonely without you I can't find a path for my feet,
Friend of my heart there are mountains between me and you.

The learned men say that love is a killing disease,
I wouldn't believe them until it had scalded my heart,
The acid is eating me I'd have done better to shun
Stabbing like mouthfuls of lightning tonight in my chest.

I met a wise woman below at the mouth of the ford,
I asked if she knew of a herb might ease love's pain,
Her voice when she answered was soft, regretful and low,
When it goes to the heart it will never come out again.

ANTHONY CRONIN

Surprise

Since we are told it we believe it's true,
Or does as it's intended. Birds eat worms,
The water flows downhill and aunts depart.
Sea heaves, sky rains and can be blue.
Always love cherishes and firelight warms.
That knocking sound you hear is just your heart.

Nothing is angry long and all surprises
Are well provided for. The dog that died
Became a legend and then had its day.
Sooner or later someone realizes
That a mistake occurred and no one lied.
If it is said to be then that's the way.

But soon when doors are opened hints are found
Of strange disorders that have no because.
In one room on the ceiling is a stain.
Someone is missing who should be around.
Some games are stopped by arbitrary laws
And an odd I does things it can't explain.

Nothing is order now and no forecast
Can be depended on since what's declared

To be may not be so and each face wears
A false expression. Yet the very last
Surprise of all still finds us unprepared:
Although we say I love you no one cares.

HUGH MAXTON

Dialectique

for Elaine

Sitting at table, or
In flight at dancing
We notice something
To happen minutely,
An event so imperceptible
As not, except for us,
To exist.

Then the world turns
An extra revolution,
A movement
In the brute routine
Lithe as grass.

Had we not seen
A shadow pass
Between balance and wit
—and recover itself!—
Heard a word
Sound as though it were

A word repeated
We were never together
At table, or
Arm on arm.

Aubrey De Vere

Song

Slanting both hands against her forehead,
On me she levelled her bright eyes;
My whole heart brightened as the sea
When midnight clouds part suddenly;
Through all my spirit went the lustre
Like starlight poured through purple skies.

And then she sang aloud, sweet music,
Yet louded as aloft it clomb;
Soft when her curving lips it left;
Then rising till the heavens were cleft,
As though each strain, on high expanding,
Were echoes in a silver dome.

But ah! she sings she does not love me;
She loves to say she ne'er can love;
To me her beauty she denies,
Bending the while on me those eyes
Whose beams might charm the mountain leopard,
Or lure Jove's herald from above!

ELEANOR HULL

The Sleep-Song of Grainne over Dermuid

From the Irish of the Poem Book of Finn

Sleep a little, a little little, thou needest feel no fear or dread,
Youth to whom my love is given, I am watching near thy head.

Sleep a little, with my blessing, Dermuid of the lightsome eye,
I will guard thee as thou dreamest, none shall harm while I am by.

Sleep, O little lamb, whose homeland was the country of the lakes,
In whose bosom torrents tremble, from whose sides the river breaks.

Sleep as slept the ancient poet, Dedach, minstrel of the South,
When he snatched from Conall Cernach Eithne of the laughing mouth.

Sleep as slept the comely Finncha 'neath the falls of Assaroe,
Who, when stately Slaine sought him, laid the Hardhead Failbe low.

Sleep in joy, as slept fair Aine, Gailan's daughter of the west,
Where, amid the flaming torches, she and Duvach found their rest.

Sleep as Degha, who in triumph, ere the sun sank o'er the land,
Stole the maiden he had craved for, plucked her from fierce Deacall's hand.

Fold of Valour, sleep a little, Glory of the Western world;
I am wondering at thy beauty, marvelling how thy locks are curled.

Like the parting of two children, bred together in one home,
Like the breaking of two spirits, if I did not see you come.

Swirl the leaves before the tempest, moans the night-wind o'er the lea,
Down its stony bed the streamlet hurries onward to the sea.

In the swaying boughs the linnet twitters in the darkling light,
On the upland wastes of heather wings the grouse its heavy flight.

In the marshland by the river sulks the otter in his den;
While the piping of the peeweet sounds across the distant fen.

On the stormy mere the wild-duck pushes outward from the brake,
With her downy brood beside her seeks the centre of the lake.

In the east the restless roe-deer bellows to his frightened hind;
On thy track the wolf-hounds gather, sniffing up against the wind.

Yet, O Dermuid, sleep a little, this one night our fear hath fled,
Youth to whom my love is given, see, I watch beside thy bed.

LOUIS MacNEICE

Cradle Song for Eleanor

Sleep, my darling, sleep;
The pity of it all
Is all we compass if
We watch disaster fall.
Put off your twenty-odd
Encumbered years and creep
Into the only heaven,
The robbers' cave of sleep.

The wild grass will whisper,
Lights of passing cars
Will streak across your dreams
And fumble at the stars;
Life will tap the window
Only too soon again,
Life will have her answer—
Do not ask her when.

When the winsome bubble
Shivers, when the bough
Breaks, will be the moment
But not here or now.

Sleep and, asleep, forget
The watchers on the wall
Awake all night who know
The pity of it all.

JAMES CLARENCE MANGAN

The Lover's Farewell

Slowly through the tomb-still streets I go—
Morn is dark, save one swart streak of gold—
Sullen rolls the far-off river's flow,
And the moon is very thin and cold.

Long and long before the house I stand
Where sleeps she, the dear, dear one I love—
All undreaming that I leave my land,
Mute and mourning, like the moon above!

Wishfully I stretch abroad mine arms
Towards the well-remembered casement-cell—
Fare thee well! Farewell thy virgin charms!
And thou stilly, stilly house, farewell!

And farewell the dear dusk little room,
Redolent of roses as a dell,
And the lattice that relieved its gloom—
And its pictured lilac walls, farewell!

Forth upon my path! I must not wait—
Bitter blows the fretful morning wind:
Warden, wilt thou softly close the gate
When thou knowest I leave my heart behind?

Eiléan Ni Chuilleanáin

From the Rose Geranium

VI

So rarely we lie
As then, in darkness
A vertical gleam relieved
Where the brilliance from outside
Struck the glass over the hearth

Breast high, if one stood,
Night lapped the bookshelves
And a dying light floated
Above us, never reaching
Us, our arrested embrace

I think at once of
That amphibious
Twilight, now that the year is
Revisiting the spring shrine
From my window the cold grey

Rectangles of stone—
February light
Spreading across the walls over my head
Washes my room with shadows, cold light until morning

ROY McFADDEN

Epithalamium

So you are married, girl. It makes me sad,
Somehow, to think of that: that you, once held
Between hot hands on slow white afternoons,
Whose eyes I knew down to their blackest depths
(Stirred by the small red smile and the white laugh)
Are married now. Some man whom I have not seen
Calls up the smile and the laugh, holds in his hands
The welcoming body, sees in the darkening eyes
Sufficient future in a smug white room.
I wish you well. May you have many sons
With darkening eyes and quiet gentle hands
To build a better future for their sons.
I, wed to history, pray for your peace,
That the smile be never twisted in your mouth,
And the pond of your mind never be rippled with sorrow:
That you may sleep your sleep as the world quakes
And never see the chasms at your feet.

EDWARD DOWDEN

Love's Chord

Stand off from me; be still your own;
Love's perfect chord maintains the sense
Through harmony, not unison,
Of finest difference.

See not as I see; set your thought
Against my thought; call up your will
To grapple mine; gay bouts we fought,
Let us be wrestlers still.

Then, if we cannot choose but mate
And mingle wholly, it will be
The doom of law, a starry fate,
And glad necessity.

LAETITIA PILKINGTON

A Song

Strephon, your breach of faith and trust
Affords me no surprise;
A man who grateful was, or just,
Might make my wonder rise.

That heart to you so fondly tied,
With pleasure wore its chain,
But from your cold neglectful pride,
Found liberty again.

For this no wrath inflames my mind,
My thanks are due to thee;
Such thanks as gen'rous victors find,
Who set their captives free.

BRENDAN KENNELLY

A Love-Song

From the Irish

Such a heart!
Should he leave, how I'd miss him.
Jewel, acorn, youth,
Kiss him!

W. B. Yeats

The Cold Heaven

Suddenly I saw the cold and rook-delighting heaven
That seemed as though ice burned and was but the more ice,
And thereupon imagination and heart were driven
So wild that every casual thought of that and this
Vanished, and left but memories, that should be out of season
With the hot blood of youth, of love crossed long ago;
And I took all the blame out of all sense and reason,
Until I cried and trembled and rocked to and fro,
Riddled with light. Ah! when the ghost begins to quicken,
Confusion of the death-bed over, is it sent
Out naked on the roads, as the books say, and stricken
By the injustice of the skies for punishment?

Valentin Iremonger

Hector

Talking to her, he knew it was the end,
The last time he'd speed her into sleep with kisses:
Achilles had it in for him and was fighting mad.
The roads of his longing she again wandered.
A girl desirable as midsummer's day.

He was a marked man and he knew it,
Being no match for Achilles whom the gods were backing.
Sadly he spoke to her for hours, his heart
Snapping like sticks, she on his shoulder crying.
Yet, sorry only that the meaning eluded him,

He slept well all night, having caressed
Andromache like a flower, though in a dream he saw
A body lying on the sands, huddled and bleeding,
Near the feet a sword in bits and by the head,
An upturned, dented helmet.

Frank O'Connor

A Learned Mistress

From the sixteenth-century Irish

Tell him it's all a lie;
I love him as much as my life;
He needn't be jealous of me—
I love him and loathe his wife.

If he kill me through jealousy now
His wife will perish of spite,
He'll die of grief for his wife—
That's three of us dead in a night.

All blessings from heaven to earth
On the head of the woman I hate,
And the man I love as my life,
Sudden death be his fate.

OLIVER ST JOHN GOGARTY

Tell Me Now

SHE

Tell me now is Love's day done?
Beauty as elect and rare
As when towns were trampled on
Lives to-day and takes the air.
Yet no amorous Triumvir
Throws the world and Rome away;
No one swims Abydos' bay;
Towns are not cast down, and none,
None begets the Moon and Sun.

HE

Do not let him hear your taunt!
Love's as strong to-day as when
Walls could not endure his brunt,
And he broke the Trojan men.
He can do as much again;
Do not doubt him for an hour,
Tempt his pleasure, not his power;
Danger gives him no affront,
He is not cooled by Hellespont.

Padraic Fallon

Mary Hynes

After the Irish of Anthony Raftery

That Sunday, on my oath, the rain was a heavy overcoat
On a poor poet, and when the rain began
In fleeces of water to buckleap like a goat
I was only a walking penance reaching Kiltartan;
And there, so suddenly that my cold spine
Broke out on the arch of my back in a rainbow,
This woman surged out of the day with so much sunlight
I was nailed there like a scarecrow,

But I found my tongue and the breath to balance it
And I said: 'If I bow to you with this hump of rain
I'll fall on my collarbone, but look, I'll chance it,
And after falling, bow again.'
She laughed, ah, she was gracious, and softly she said to me,
'For all your lovely talking I go marketing with an ass,
I'm no hill-queen, alas, or Ireland, that grass widow,
So hurry on, sweet Raftery, or you'll keep me late for Mass!'

The parish priest has blamed me for missing second Mass
And the bell talking on the rope of the steeple,
But the tonsure of the poet is the bright crash

Of love that blinds the irons on his belfry,
Were I making an Aisling I'd tell the tale of her hair,
But now I've grown careful of my listeners
So I pass over one long day and the rainy air
Where we sheltered in whispers.

When we left the dark evening at last outside her door,
She lighted a lamp though a gaming company
Could have sighted each trump by the light of her unshawled poll,
And indeed she welcomed me
With a big quart bottle and I mooned there over glasses
Till she took that bird, the phoenix, from the spit;
And 'Raftery', says she, 'a feast is no bad dowry,
Sit down now and taste it!'

If I praised Ballylea before it was only for the mountains
Where I broke horses and ran wild,
And not for its seven crooked smoky houses
Where seven crones are tied
All day to the listening top of a half door,
And nothing to be heard or seen
But the drowsy dropping of water
And a gander on the green.

But, Boys! I was blind as a kitten till last Sunday.
This town is earth's very navel!
Seven palaces are thatched there of a Monday,
And O the seven queens whose pale

Proud faces with their seven glimmering sisters,
The Pleiads, light the evening where they stroll,
And one can find the well by their wet footprints,
And make one's soul;

For Mary Hynes, rising, gathers up there
Her ripening body from all the love stories;
And, rinsing herself at morning, shakes her hair
And stirs the old gay books in libraries;
And what shall I do with sweet Boccaccio?
And shall I send Ovid back to school again
With a new headline for his copybook,
And a new pain?

Like a nun she will play you a sweet tune on a spinet,
And from such grasshopper music leap
Like Herod's hussy who fancied a saint's head
For grace after meat;
Yet she'll peg out a line of clothes on a windy morning
And by noonday put them ironed in the chest,
And you'll swear by her white fingers she does nothing
But take her fill of rest.

And I'll wager now that my song is ended,
Loughrea, that old dead city where the weavers
Have pined at the mouldering looms since Helen broke the thread,
Will be piled again with silver fleeces:
O the new coats and big horses! The raving and the ribbons!

And Ballylea in hubbub and uproar!
And may Raftery be dead if he's not there to ruffle it
On his own mare, Shank's mare, that never needs a spur!

But, ah, Sweet Light, though your face coins
My heart's very metals, isn't it folly without pardon
For Raftery to sing so that men, east and west, come
Spying on your vegetable garden?
We could be so quiet in your chimney corner—
Yet how could a poet hold you any more than the sun,
Burning in the big bright hazy heart of harvest,
Could be tied in a henrun?

Bless your poet then and let him go!
He'll never stack a haggard with his breath:
His thatch of words will not keep rain or snow
Out of the house, or keep back death.
But Raftery, rising, curses as he sees you
Stir the fire and wash delph,
That he was bred a poet whose selfish trade it is
To keep no beauty to himself.

C. DAY-LEWIS

Jig

That winter love spoke and we raised no objection, at
Easter 'twas daisies all light and affectionate,
June sent us crazy for natural selection—not
Four traction-engines could tear us apart.
Autumn then coloured the map of our land,
Oaks shuddered and apples came ripe to the hand,
In the gap of the hills we played happily, happily,
Even the moon couldn't tell us apart.

Grave winter drew near and said, 'This will not do at all—
If you continue, I fear you will rue it all.'
So at the New Year we vowed to eschew it
Although we both knew it would break our heart.
But spring made hay of our good resolutions—
Lovers, you may be as wise as Confucians,
Yet once love betrays you he plays you and plays you
Like fishes for ever, so take it to heart.

Maura Dooley

At Les Deux Magots

The bloom on the fruit is perfect.
His moist eyes are fixed on her.
As he hands her plums she thinks
he is the kind of man who'd kiss her
on the lips in friendship,
to whom she'd try to turn a cheek in time.
The way he gives me ripeness
when what I want is something raw.

An old memory makes the blood
rock in her veins: Ford, in the street,
face turned from her, arms filled with books,
the back of his crow-black coat resolute,
that moment, polished like a piece of bone.
Her thoughts are all crooked now,
her hands cold in their thin cotton gloves
She takes the plums from him dumbly.

J. M. Synge

The Masque of May

The chiffchaff and celandine
The blackbird and the bee
The chestnut branches topped with green
Have met my love and me
And we have played the masque of May
So sweet and commonplace and gay
The sea's first miracle of blue
Bare trees that glitter near the sky
Grow with a love and longing new
Where went my love and I
And there we played the masque of May
So old and infinite and gay.

Thomas Moore

Thee, Thee, Only Thee

The dawning of morn, the daylight's sinking,
The night's long hours still find me thinking
Of thee, thee, only thee.
When friends are met, and goblets crowned,
And smiles are near that once enchanted,
Unreached by all that sunshine round,
My soul, like some dark spot, is haunted
By thee, thee, only thee.

Whatever in fame's high path could waken
My spirit once is now forsaken
For thee, thee, only thee.
Like shores by which some headlong bark
To the ocean hurries, resting never,
Life's scenes go by me, bright or dark
I know not, heed not, hastening ever
To thee, thee, only thee.

I have not a joy but of thy bringing,
And pain itself seems sweet when springing
From thee, thee, only thee.
Like spells that nought on earth can break,

Till lips that know the charm have spoken,
This heart, howe'er the world may wake
Its grief, its scorn, can but be broken
By thee, thee, only thee.

THOMAS MOORE

Love's Young Dream

The days are gone, when beauty bright
My heart's chain wove;
When my dream of life, from morn till night,
Was love, still love.

New hope may bloom,
And days may come,
Of milder, calmer beam;
But there's nothing half so sweet in life
As love's young dream.

FERGUS ALLEN

Way Back Then

The floor-show ends, lights dim, I tilt the bottle;
The maestro turns, vibrant in black and white,
Confers the boon of his electric ego
And drives the music forward through the night.

So here I sit, champagne glass in my hand,
Afloat on rhythms of the Latin south,
Drawn by inexorable tidal currents
To the pearl harbour of your smiling mouth.

Sir Samuel Ferguson

Deirdre's Lament for the Sons of Usnach

From the Irish

The lions of the hill are gone,
And I am left alone—alone—
Dig the grave both wide and deep,
For I am sick, and fain would sleep!

The falcons of the wood are flown,
And I am left alone—alone—
Dig the grave both deep and wide,
And let us slumber side by side.

The dragons of the rock are sleeping,
Sleep that wakes not for our weeping;
Dig the grave and make it ready;
Lay me on my true-love's body.

Lay their spears and bucklers bright
By the warriors' side aright;
Many a day the three before me
On their linkèd bucklers bore me.

Lay upon the low grave floor,
'Neath each head, the blue claymore;
Many a time the noble three
Redden'd these blue blades for me.

Lay the collars, as is meet,
Of their greyhounds at their feet;
Many a time for me have they
Brought the tall red deer to bay.

In the falcon's jesses throw,
Hook and arrow, line and bow;
Never again by stream or plain
Shall the gentle woodsmen go.

Sweet companions ye were ever—
Harsh to me, your sister, never;
Woods and wilds and misty valleys
Were, with you, as good's a palace.

Oh! to hear my true love singing,
Sweet as sound of trumpets ringing;
Like the sway of ocean swelling
Roll'd his deep voice round our dwelling.

Oh! to hear the echoes pealing
Round our green and fairy sheeling,

When the three, with soaring chorus,
Pass'd the silent skylark o'er us.

Echo now, sleep, morn and even—
Lark alone enchant the heaven!—
Ardan's lips are scant of breath,
Naisi's tongue is cold in death.

Stag, exult on glen and mountain—
Salmon, leap from loch to fountain—
Heron, in the free air warm ye—
Usnach's sons no more will harm ye!

Erin's stay no more you are,
Rulers of the ridge of war;
Nevermore 'twill be your fate
To keep the beam of battle straight!

Woe is me! by fraud and wrong,
Traitors false and tyrants strong,
Fell clan Usnach, bought and sold,
For Barach's feast and Conor's gold!

Woe to Eman, roof and wall!
Woe to Red Branch, hearth and hall!—
Tenfold woe and black dishonour
To the foul and false clan Conor!

Dig the grave both wide and deep,
Sick I am and fain would sleep!
Dig the grave and make it ready,
Lay me on my true-love's body!

FRANCES WYNNE

Nocturne

The long day was bright,
It slowly passed from the purple slopes of the hill;
And then the night
Came floating quietly down, and the world grew still.

Now I lie awake,
The south wind stirs the white curtains to and fro.
Cries the corncrake
In fields that stretch by the stream-side, misty and low.

At the meadow's edge
I know the faint pink clover is heavy with dew.
Under the hedge
The speedwell closes its sweet eyes, dreamily blue.

With pursed rosy lips
The baby buds are asleep on the apple tree.
The river slips
Beneath the scarcely swayed willows, on to the sea.

The dark grows, and grows,
But I'm too happy to sleep, and the reason why
No creature knows,
Save certain little brown birds, and my love, and I.

Hugh Maxton

On Failing to Translate

The rain had stopped maybe an hour ago.
We stood alone in the sodden garden
Waiting to go home or be driven
To some other furious hope.
Exhaust fumes lay at the bottom of the road
Grey upon grey, a carpet in a showroom.

Then I heard, suddenly as if it had started
To life, the rain still falling in the grass
Dropping between the blades and the leaves
With a motion which I knew must startle us.
And I said 'This is love's benediction
And nothing more.' The hands we held
Shaking in farewell were a bridge between

Us, pushing against either bank, a strength
Delicately equal to ours, but resisting always.

The water beneath us bubbled downwards
On its long journey back to the earth.

ELEANOR HULL

The Stars Stand Up

From the Irish

The stars stand up in the air,
The sun and the moon are set,
The sea that ebbed dry of its tide
Leaves no single pebble wet;
The cuckoo keeps saying each hour
That she, my Storeen, is fled,—
O Girl of the brave, free tresses,
Far better had you struck me dead!

Three things have I learned through love,
Sorrow, and death, and pain,
My mind reminding me daily
I never shall see you again;
You left me no cure for my sickness,
Yet I pray, though my night be long,—
My sharp grief! and my heart is broken,—
That God may forgive your wrong.

She was sweeter than fiddle and lute,
Or the shining of grass through the dew,
She was soft as the blackbird's flute

When the light of the day is new;
From her feet on the lone hill-top
I have heard the honey dropping;
Why, Girl, did you come to my door?
Or why could you not be stopping?

George Darley

Song

From Sylva

The streams that wind amid the hills,
And lost in pleasure slowly roam,
While their deep joy the valley fills,
Ev'n these will leave their mountain-home:
So may it, love! with others be,
But I will never wend from thee!

The leaf forsakes the parent spray,
The blossom quits the stem as fast
The rose-enamoured bird will stray,
And leave his eglantine at last;
So may it, love! with others be,
But I will never wend from thee!

SEAMUS HEANEY

Bedside Reading

The whole place airier. Big summer trees
Stirring at eye level when we waken
And little shoots of ivy creeping in
Unless they've been trained out—like memories
You've trained so long now they can show their face
And keep their distance. White-mouthed depression
Swims out from its shadow like a dolphin
With wet, unreadable, unfurtive eyes.

I swim in Homer. In Book Twenty-three
At last Odysseus and Penelope
Waken together. One bedpost of the bed
Is the living trunk of an old olive tree
And is their secret. As ours could have been ivy,
Evergreen, atremble and unsaid.

BRENDAN KENNELLY

Wings

The words have been said.
He towers above her, she pretends he's not there,
She concentrates on washing a heart of lettuce,
Wet leaves glitter in her fingers.
He folds his hand like wings about her black hair
And kisses her head.

ELEANOR HULL

The Shining Posy

From the Irish of Anthony Raftery

There is a bright posy on the edge of the quay
And she far beyond Deirdre with her pleasant ways
Or if I would say Helen, the queen of the Greeks,
On whose account hundreds have fallen at Troy.
The flame and the white in her mingled together,
And sweeter her mouth than cuckoo on the bough,
And the way she has with her, where will you find them
Since died the pearl that was in Ballylaoi?

If you were to see the sky-maiden decked out
On a fine sunny day in the street, and she walking,
The light shining out from her snow-white bosom
Would give sight of the eyes to a sightless man.
The love of hundreds is on her brow,
The sight of her as the gleam of the Star of Doom;
If she had been there in the time of the gods
It is not to Venus the apple would have gone.

Her hair falling with her down to her knees,
Twining and curling to the mouth of her shoe;
Her parted locks, with the grey of the dew on them,

And her curls sweeping after her on the road;
She is the coolun is brightest and most mannerly
Of all who ever opened eye or who lived in life;
And if the country of Lord Lucan were given me,
By the strength of my cause, the jewel should be mine.

Her form slender, chalk-white, her cheeks like roses,
And her breasts rounded over against her heart;
Her neck and her brow and her auburn hair,
She stands before us like the dew of harvest.
Virgil, Cicero, nor the power of Homer,
Would not bring any to compare with her bloom and gentle ways;
O Blossom of Youth, I am guilty with desire of you,
And unless you come to me I shall not live a month.

Walking or dancing, if you were to see the fair shoot,
It is to the Flower of the Branches you would give your love,
Her face alight, and her heart without sorrow,
And were it not pleasant to be in her company?
The greatness of Samson or Alexander
I would not covet, surely, in place of my desire;
And if I do not get leave to talk to Mary Staunton
I am in doubt that short will be my life.

She bade me 'Good-morrow' early, with kindness,
She set a stool for me, and not in the corner,
She drank a drink with me, she was the heart of hospitality,
At the time that I rose up to go on my way.

I fell to talking and discoursing with her,
It was mannerly she looked at me, the apple-blossom,
And here is my word of mouth to you, without falsehood,
That I have left the branch with her from Mary Brown.

Patrick Kavanagh

Bluebells for Love

There will be bluebells growing under the big trees
And you will be there and I will be there in May;
For some other reason we both will have to delay
The evening in Dunshaughlin—to please
Some imagined relation,
So both of us came to walk through that plantation.

We will be interested in the grass,
In an old bucket-hoop, in the ivy that weaves
Green incongruity among dead leaves,
We will put on surprise at carts that pass—
Only sometimes looking sideways at the bluebells in the plantation
And never frighten them with too wild an exclamation.

We will be wise, we will not let them guess
That we are watching them or they will pose
A mere façade like boys
Caught out in virtue's naturalness.
We will not impose on the bluebells in that plantation
Too much of our desire's adulation.

We will have other loves—or so they'll think;
The primroses or the ferns or the briars,

Or even the rusty paling wires,
Or the violets on the sunless sorrel bank.
Only as an aside the bluebells in the plantation
Will mean a thing to our dark contemplation.

We'll know love little by little, glance by glance.
Ah, the clay under these roots is so brown!
We'll steal from Heaven while God is in the town—
I caught an angel smiling in a chance
Look through the tree-trunks of the plantation
As you and I walked slowly to the station.

KUNO MEYER

The Song of Crede, Daughter of Guare

From the Irish, probably tenth century

These are arrows that murder sleep
At every hour in the bitter-cold night:
Pangs of love throughout the day
For the company of the man from Roiny.

Great love of a man from another land
Has come to me beyond all else:
It has taken my bloom, no colour is left,
It does not let me rest.

Sweeter than songs was his speech,
Save holy adoration of Heaven's King;
He was a glorious flame, no boastful word fell from his lips,
A slender mate for a maid's side.

When I was a child I was bashful,
I was not given to going to trysts:
Since I have come to a wayward age,
My wantonness has beguiled me.

I have every good with Guare,
The King of cold Aidne:
But my mind has fallen away from my people
To the meadow at Irluachair.

There is chanting in the meadow of glorious Aidne
Around the sides of Colman's Church:
Glorious flame, now sunk into the grave—
Dinertach was his name.

It wrings my pitiable heart, O chaste Christ,
What has fallen to my lot:
These are arrows that murder sleep
At every hour in the bitter-cold night.

KEVIN FALLER

Like Seals from Sleep

They slid like seals from sleep
To the bed's small beach,
And on that desolation
Turned each to each;
The shock of touch recalled
Terrible fables of humanity,
The gods of good and evil,
The rods of eternity:

They slid down again—
A trembling gleam—
To the dark tide and left
The human dream.

LOUIS MACNEICE

The Introduction

They were introduced in a grave glade
And she frightened him because she was young
And thus too late. Crawly crawly
Went the twigs above their heads and beneath
The grass beneath their feet the larvae
Split themselves laughing. Crawly crawly
Went the cloud above the treetops reaching
For a sun that lacked the nerve to set
And he frightened her because he was old
And thus too early. Crawly crawly
Went the string quartet that was tuning up
In the back of the mind. You two should have met
Long since, he said, or else not now.
The string quartet in the back of the mind
Was all tuned up with nowhere to go.
They were introduced in a green grave.

RICHARD BRINSLEY SHERIDAN

Thou Canst Not Boast of Fortune's Store

Thou canst not boast of Fortune's store,
My love, while me they wealthy call:
But I was glad to find thee poor,
For with my heart I'd give thee all.
And then the grateful youth shall own
I loved him for himself alone.

But when his worth my hand shall gain,
No word or look of mine shall show
That I the smallest thought retain
Of what my bounty did bestow:
Yet still his grateful heart shall own
I loved him for himself alone.

OLIVER ST JOHN GOGARTY

Leda and the Swan

Though her Mother told her
Not to go a-bathing,
Leda loved the river
And she could not keep away:
Wading in its freshets
When the noon was heavy;
Walking by the water
At the close of day.

Where between its waterfalls,
Underneath the beeches,
Gently flows a broader
Hardly moving stream,
And the balanced trout lie
In the quiet reaches;
Taking all her clothes off,
Leda went to swim.

There was not a flag-leaf
By the river's margin
That might be a shelter
From a passer-by;
And a sudden whiteness
In the quiet darkness,

Let alone the splashing,
Was enough to catch an eye.

But the place was lonely,
And her clothes were hidden;
Even cattle walking
In the ford had gone away;
Every single farm-hand
Sleeping after dinner,—
What's the use of talking?
There was no one in the way.

In, without a stitch on,
Peaty water yielded,
Till her head was lifted
With its ropes of hair;
It was more surprising
Than a lily gilded,
Just to see how golden
Was her body there:

Lolling in the water,
Lazily uplifting
Limbs that on the surface
Whitened into snow;
Leaning on the water,
Indolently drifting,
Hardly any faster
Than the foamy bubbles go.

You would say to see her
Swimming in the lonely
Pool, or after, dryer,
Putting on her clothes:
'O but she is lovely,
Not a soul to see her,
And how lovely only
Leda's Mother knows!'

Under moving branches
Leisurely she dresses,
And the leafy sunlight
Made you wonder were
All its woven shadows
But her golden tresses,
Or a smock of sunlight
For her body bare.

When on earth great beauty
Goes exempt from danger,
It will be endangered
From a source on high;
When unearthly stillness
Falls on leaves, the ranger,
In his wood-lore anxious,
Gazes at the sky.

While her hair was drying,
Came a gentle languor,

Whether from the bathing
Or the breeze she didn't know.
Anyway she lay there,
And her Mother's anger
(Worse if she had wet hair)
Could not make her dress and go.

Whitest of all earthly
Things, the white that's rarest,
Is the snow on mountains
Standing in the sun;
Next the clouds above them,
Then the down is fairest
On the breast and pinions
Of a proudly sailing swan.

And she saw him sailing
On the pool where lately
She had stretched unnoticed,
As she thought, and swum;
And she never wondered
Why, erect and stately,
Where no river weed was
Such a bird had come.

What was it she called him:
Goosey-goosey gander?
For she knew no better
Way to call a swan;

And the bird responding
Seemed to understand her,
For he left his sailing
For the bank to waddle on.

Apple blossoms under
Hills of Lacedaemon,
With the snow beyond them
In the still blue air,
To the swan who hid them
With his wings asunder,
Than the breasts of Leda,
Were not lovelier!

Of the tales that daughters
Tell their poor old mothers,
Which by all accounts are
Often very odd;
Leda's was a story
Stranger than all others.
What was there to say but:
Glory be to God?

And she half-believed her,
For she knew her daughter;
And she saw the swan-down
Tangled in her hair.
Though she knew how deeply

Runs the stillest water,
How could she protect her
From the wingèd air?

Why is it effects are
Greater than their causes?
Why should causes often
Differ from effects?
Why should what is lovely
Fill the world with harness?
And the most deceived be
She who least suspects?

When the hyacinthine
Eggs were in the basket,
Blue as at the whiteness
Where a cloud begins;
Who would dream there lay there
All that Trojan brightness;
Agamemnon murdered;
And the mighty Twins?

CHARLES G. HALPINE

Quakerdom (The Formal Call)

Through her forced, abnormal quiet
Flashed the soul of frolic riot,
And a most malicious laughter lighted up her downcast eyes;
All in vain I tried each topic,
Ranged from polar climes to tropic,—
Every commonplace I started met with yes-or-no replies.

For her mother—stiff and stately,
As if starched and ironed lately—
Sat erect, with rigid elbows bedded thus in curving palms;
There she sat on guard before us,
And in words precise, decorous,
And most calm, reviewed the weather, and recited several psalms.

How without abruptly ending
This my visit, and offending
Wealthy neighbors, was the problem which employed my mental care;
When the butler, bowing lowly,
Uttered clearly, stiffly, slowly,
'Madam, please, the gardener wants you,'—
Heaven, I thought, has heard my prayer.

'Pardon me!' she grandly uttered;
Bowing low I gladly muttered,
'Surely, madam,' and, relieved, I turned to scan the daughter's face:
Ha! what pent-up mirth outflashes
From beneath those penciled lashes!
How the drill of Quaker custom yields to Nature's brilliant grace.

Brightly springs the prisoned fountain
From the side of Delphis mountain
When the stone that weighed upon its buoyant life is thrust aside;
So the long-enforced stagnation
Of the maiden's conversation
Now imparted five-fold brilliance to its ever-varying tide.

Widely ranging, quickly changing,
Witty, winning, from beginning
Unto end I listened, merely flinging in a casual word:
Eloquent, and yet how simple!
Hand and eye, and eddying dimple,
Tongue and lip together made a music seen as well as heard.

When the noonday woods are ringing,
All the birds of summer singing,
Suddenly there falls a silence, and we know a serpent nigh:
So upon the door a rattle
Stopped our animated tattle,
And the stately mother found us prim enough to suit her eye.

Anonymous

The Red Man's Wife

From the Irish, translated by Douglas Hyde

'Tis what they say,
Thy little heel fits in a shoe.
'Tis what they say,
Thy little mouth kisses well, too.
'Tis what they say,
Thousand loves that you leave me to rue;
That the tailor went the way
That the wife of the Red man knew.

Nine months did I spend
In a prison penned tightly and bound;
Bolts on my smalls
And a thousand locks frowning around;
But o'er the tide
I would leap with the leap of a swan,
Could I once set my side
By the bride of the Red-haired man.

I thought, O my life,
That one house between us, love, would be;
And I thought I would find

You once coaxing my child on your knee;
But now the curse of the High One,
On him let it be,
And on all of the band of the liars
Who put silence between you and me.

There grows a tree in the garden
With blossoms that tremble and shake,
I lay my hands on its bark
And I feel that my heart must break.
On one wish alone
My soul through the long months ran,
One little kiss
From the wife of the Red-haired man.

But the Day of Doom shall come,
And hills and harbours be rent;
A mist shall fall on the sun
From the dark clouds heavily sent;
The sea shall be dry,
And earth under mourning and ban;
Then loud shall he cry
For the wife of the Red-haired man.

Richard Murphy

Moonshine

To think
I must be alone:
To love
We must be together.

I think I love you
When I'm alone
More than I think of you
When we're together.

I cannot think
Without loving
Or love
Without thinking.

Alone I love
To think of us together
Together I think
I'd love to be alone.

Thomas Kinsella

Tête à Tête

Try subtlety. 'I was in love all May
Not with you, really, but with You in Me.'

Better a blunt avowal. Hour by hour
One wrong response contaminates the air.

She loves . . . A web of doubt confused her sight
And silenced the window-table where they sat;

His fingers whitened on the trembling cup.
. . . *And I, as long as bantering passions keep.*

A complex wish to guide her altered to
A mild compunction as she poured his tea.

Their happiness when they forgave each other
Made neither ready to have faith in either.

Life is change and yields its deference
Not to good nor ill, but difference.

Last time they spoke it was of fumbled leaving;
The station deafening, the winter living.

THOMAS MOORE

Did Not

'Twas a new feeling—something more
Than we had dared to own before,
Which then we hid not;
We saw it in each other's eye,
And wished, in every half-breathed sigh,
To speak, but did not.

She felt my lips' impassioned touch—
'Twas the first time I dared so much,
And yet she chid not;
But whispered o'er my burning brow,
'Oh, do you doubt I love you now?'
Sweet soul! I did not.

Warmly I felt her bosom thrill,
I pressed it closer, closer still,
Though gently bid not;
Till—oh! the world hath seldom heard
Of lovers, who so nearly erred,
And yet, who did not.

GABRIEL FITZMAURICE

Entanglement

From the Irish of Caitlin Maude

Walk, my love,
by the strand tonight—
walk, and away
with tears—
arise and walk tonight

henceforth never bend your knee
at that mountain grave
those flowers have withered
and my bones decayed . . .

(I speak to you tonight
from the bottom of the sea—
I speak to you each night
from the bottom of the sea . . .)

once I walked on the strand—
I walked to the tide's edge—
wave played with wave—
the white foam licked my feet—
I slowly raised my eye

and there far out on the deep
in the tangle of foam and wave
I saw the loneliness in your eye
the sorrow in your face

I walked out on the deep
from knee to waist
and from waist to shoulder
until I was swallowed
in sorrow and loneliness

BRENDAN KENNELLY

A Restoration

Was it the lazy haze of the summer afternoon
Drifting into her, or the warm
Indolence of the sea caressing every bone
That made her stretch out on the sandy grass
And give herself into the arms
Of this prolonged, seductive moment?
Was she free a while of children's cries
Boring through her, shrill and insistent?
Whatever it was, she suddenly knew she was naked
And glancing at her left hand
Saw her marriage ring was missing.
She was panic as she searched and searched
Until she found it in the thieving ground
And restored it to its mark, dark and shining.

John Todhunter

A Moment

'Was that the wind?' she said,
And turned her head
To where, on a green bank, the primrose flowers
Seemed with new beauty suddenly endowed,
As though they gazed out of their mortal cloud
On things unseen, communing with strange powers.

Then upon that green place
Fell a new grace,
As when a sun-gleam visits drops of dew,
And every drop shines like a mystic gem,
Set in the front of morning's diadem,
With hues more tender than e'er a diamond knew.

And something seemed to pass—
As through the grass
The presence of the gentlest wind will go—
Delicately through her bosom and her hair,
Till, with delight, she found herself more fair,
And her heart sang, unutterably low.

John Swanwick Drennan

Not Gone Yet

'Wave ye, dark tresses! clustering or apart,
Contrast your beauty with the snowy brow;
Ringlets no more are fetters to my heart,
Nor doth it tremble with their motion now.
Smile, ye bright eyes! Your wanton beams no more
Shall wrongfully divert a glance of mine;
My bark is turned from Love's illusive shore,
And its false lights now unregarded shine.'
But whilst the mariner in boastful joy,
Again afloat, his sails is shaking out,
Lo! at the helm there stands a Winged Boy,
And silently the ship is put about.

PAUL DURCAN

The Difficulty That Is Marriage

We disagree to disagree, we divide, we differ;
Yet each night as I lie in bed beside you
And you are faraway curled up in sleep
I array the moonlit ceiling with a mosaic of question-marks;
How was it I was so lucky to have ever met you?
I am no brave pagan proud of my mortality
Yet gladly on this changeling earth I should live for ever
If it were with you, my sleeping friend.
I have my troubles, and I shall always have them
But I should rather live with you for ever
Than exchange my troubles for a changeless kingdom.
But I do not put you on a pedestal or throne;
You must have your faults but I do not see them.
If it were with you, I should live for ever.

J. M. SYNGE

In Kerry

We heard the thrushes by the shore and sea,
And saw the golden stars' nativity,
Then round we went the lane by Thomas Flynn,
Across the church where bones lie out and in;
And there I asked beneath a lonely cloud
Of strange delight, with one bird singing loud,
What change you'd wrought in graveyard, rock and sea,
This new wild paradise to wake for me . . .
Yet knew no more than knew these merry sins
Had built this stack of thigh-bones, jaws and shins.

FRANK O'CONNOR

Exile

From the Irish

What happier fortune can one find
Than with the girl who pleased one's mind
To leave one's home and friends behind
And sail on the first favouring wind?

LADY GREGORY

What Have I Gained?

What have I gained? A little charity?
I never more may dare to fling a stone
Or say of any weakness I may see
That I more strength and wisdom would have shown—
And I have learned in love lore to be wise:
And knowledge of the evil and the good
Have had one moment's glimpse of Paradise
And know the flavour of forbidden food.
But this, if it be gold has much alloy,
And I would gladly all the past undo
Were it not for the thought that brings me joy
That I once made some happiness for you—
That sometimes in a dark and troubled hour
I had, like Jesse's son, a soothing power.

AE

Illusion

What is the love of shadowy lips
That know not what they seek or press,
From whom the lure for ever slips
And fails their phantom tenderness?

The mystery and light of eyes
That near to mine grow dim and cold;
They move afar in ancient skies
'Mid flame and mystic darkness rolled.

O beauty, as thy heart o'erflows
In tender yielding unto me,
A vast desire awakes and grows
Unto forgetfulness of thee.

Samuel Lover

What Will You Do, Love?

'What will you do, love, when I am going,
With white sail flowing, the seas beyond,
What will you do, love, when waves divide us,
And friends may chide us for being fond?'
'Tho' waves divide us, and friends be chiding,
In faith abiding, I'll still be true,
And I'll pray for thee on the stormy ocean
In deep devotion—that's what I'll do.'

'What would you do, love, if distant tidings,
Thy fond confidings should undermine;
And I, abiding 'neath sultry skies
Should think other eyes were as bright as thine?'
'Oh! name it not! though guilt and shame
Were on thy name, I'd still be true!
But that heart of thine, should another share it,
I could not bear it—what would I do?'

'What would you do, love, when home returning,
With hopes high burning, with wealth for you,
If my barque which bounded o'er foreign foam,
Should be lost near home—ah! what would you do?'

'So thou wert spared, I'd bless the morrow,
In want and sorrow, that left me you!
And I'd welcome thee from the wasting billow,
This heart thy pillow—that's what I'd do.'

AUSTIN CLARKE

The Planter's Daughter

When night stirred at sea
And the fire brought a crowd in,
They say that her beauty
Was music in mouth
And few in the candlelight
Thought her too proud,
For the house of the planter
Is known by the trees.

Men that had seen her
Drank deep and were silent,
The women were speaking
Wherever she went—
As a bell that is rung
Or a wonder told shyly,
And O she was the Sunday
In every week.

Thomas Parnell

Song

When thy beauty appears
In its graces and airs,
All bright as an angel new dropt from the sky;
At distance I gaze, and am awed by my fears,
So strangely you dazzle my eye!

But when without art,
Your kind thoughts you impart,
When your love runs in blushes through every vein;
When it darts from your eyes, when it pants in your heart,
Then I know you're a woman again.

There's a passion and pride
In our sex, (she replied,)
And thus (might I gratify both) I would do:
Still an angel appear to each lover beside,
But still be a woman to you.

MARY BARBER

Advice to Her Son on Marriage

From *The Conclusion of a Letter to the Rev. Mr C—*

When you gain her Affection, take care to preserve it;
Lest others persuade her, you do not deserve it.
Still study to heighten the Joys of her Life;
Not treat her the worse, for her being your Wife.
If in Judgment she errs, set her right, without Pride:
'Tis the Province of insolent Fools, to deride.
A Husband's first Praise, is a Friend and Protector
Then change not these Titles, for Tyrant and Hector.
Let your Person be neat, unaffectedly clean,
Tho' alone with your wife the whole Day you remain.
Chuse Books, for her study, to fashion her Mind,
To emulate those who excell'd of her Kind.
Be Religion the principal Care of your Life,
As you hope to be blest in your Children and Wife:
So you, in your Marriage, shall gain its true End;
And find, in your Wife, a Companion and Friend.

SEAMUS HEANEY

The Otter

When you plunged
The light of Tuscany wavered
And swung through the pool
From top to bottom

I loved your wet head and smashing crawl,
Your fine swimmer's back and shoulders
Surfacing and surfacing again
This year and every year since.

I sat dry-throated on the warm stones.
You were beyond me.
The mellowed clarities, the grace-deep air
Thinned and disappointed.

Thank God for the slow loadening.
When I hold you now
We are close and deep
As the atmosphere on water.

My two hands are plumbed water.
You are my palpable, lithe

Otter of memory
In the pool of the moment,

Turning to swim on your back,
Each silent, thigh-shaking kick
Re-tilting the light
Heaving the cool at your neck.

And suddenly you're out
Back again, intent as ever,
Heavy and frisky in your freshened pelt
Printing the stones.

GABRIEL ROSENSTOCK

The Search

For my wife, Eithne
From his own Irish poem

I

Where are the poems I promised
I would write for you?
They are not in ink—

You will find them in the foam of rivers
In the seas
In the vapour above clifftops
In the swirling breeze
In eagles' eyes
In the clouds
In the skies
Even in the stars.
They're on their eternal journey
From void to void.
They are not in print—
The flowers' sweetness snatched them
While you hunkered in the garden.
Nettles burned them
Dock soothed them

Ladybirds landed on them
And walked like critics
Seeking rhyme and metre.
They even failed to find a title. For who
Could put a name on you!
And yet each day I name you
With every breath.
Where are all the verbs?
You have gathered them to yourself.
The adjectives?
Nestling in your breast.
Punctuation?
It adorns you.
Nouns, vowels, consonants,
The Irish language, its sound and sense,
I dedicate to you, Eithne.

II

From age to age I seek your shape
Like a winglet
Like a leaf.
When we are children,
Heroes,
and elders,
On death's cold stone
And in the womb,

Every moment
Shapes my poem—
It ever welcomes you.
Can you hear the gale?
The world turns
And all is turning,
The hills and the peaks above them.
We closed our eyes, and opened them,
Then closed them again in wonder.

III

Do not greet me
Do not look at me
Do not seek me
I escape
I seek you
We do not exist
In any time
In any place
We are not in the realms of words
Or love
(Although our love is strong).
Take my hand,
Love; hear the heart's tympany
That beat long ago for you and me,
That we still don't understand.

CAROLINE ELIZABETH SARAH NORTON

Sonnet

Where the red wine-cup floweth, there art thou!
Where luxury curtains out the evening sky;—
Triumphant Mirth sits flush'd upon thy brow,
And ready laughter lurks within thine eye.
Where the long day declineth, lone I sit,
In idle thought, my listless hands entwined,
And, faintly smiling at remember'd wit,
Act the scene over to my musing mind.
In my lone dreams I hear thy eloquent voice,
I see the pleased attention of the throng,
And bid my spirit in thy joy rejoice,
Lest in love's selfishness I do thee wrong.
Ah! midst that proud and mirthful company
Send'st *thou* no wondering thought to love and me?

Robin Flower

He Praises His Wife

From the Irish

White hands of languorous grace,
Fair feet of stately pace
And snowy-shining knees—
My love was made of these.

Stars glimmered in her hair,
Slim was she, satin-fair,
Dark like seal's fur her brows
Shadowed her cheek's fresh rose.

What words can match its worth,
That beauty closed in earth,
That courteous, stately air,
Winsome and shy and fair.

To have known all this and be
Tortured with memory
—Curse on this waking breath—
Makes me in love with death.

Better to sleep than see
This house now dark to me
A lonely shell in place
Of that unrivalled grace.

Brian MacGuigan

Contentment

Why am I
So intractably intact?
Where are the loose ends
Of spawned off ecstasies,
The hidden terrors,
The secret fears
Which used to occupy my mind?

All gone
Like seed in winter
Or a moon's ray at dawn;

Contentment nestles me,
In its womb I lie
Foetal and unthinking,
Sun blessed,
Love kissed,
Trapped by a thousand meaningless intimacies.

Samuel Beckett

Cascando

1

why not merely the despaired of
occasion of
wordshed

is it not better abort than be barren

the hours after you are gone are so leaden
they will always start dragging too soon
the grapples clawing blindly the bed of want
bringing up the bones the old loves
sockets filled once with eyes like yours
all always is it better too soon than never
the black want splashing their faces
saying again nine days never floated the loved
nor nine months
nor nine lives

2

saying again
if you do not teach me I shall not learn

saying again there is a last
even of last times
last times of begging
last times of loving
of knowing not knowing pretending
a last even of last times of saying
if you do not love me I shall not be loved
if I do not love you I shall not love

the churn of stale words in the heart again
love love love thud of the old plunger
pestling the unalterable
whey of words
terrified again
of not loving
of loving and not you
of being loved and not by you
of knowing not knowing pretending
pretending

I and all the others that will love you
if they love you

3

unless they love you

LADY GREGORY

Will You Be as Hard?

From the Irish of Douglas Hyde

Will you be as hard?
Will you be as hard,
Colleen, as you are quiet?
Will you be without pity
On me for ever?
Listen to me, Noireen,
Listen, aroon;
Put healing on me
From your quiet mouth.
I am in the little road
That is dark and narrow,
The little road that has led
Thousands to sleep

Vincent O'Sullivan

By the Sea-Wall

Wing thy race when the night comes down,
My cream-white bird with the scarlet mouth,
Fly to my dear in the sea-walled town,
Where she dreams her life in the soundless south:
Nestle thee close to her yearning breast
With a flutter of wings and a frightened stare,
And all the love-notes she loveth best
Breathe there! Breathe there!
My cream-white bird with the scarlet mouth.

Out from the fog on the cold sea-wall,
The death-witch comes with her ruined hands;
The thread of her voice is thin and small,
Yet it whines afar over goodly lands!
God have thee in keeping, my cream-white bird,
My gentle queen lulled in love's mysteries,—
God help thee! the tune of thy voice she has heard
She sees! She sees!
The gaunt death-witch with the ruined hands.

She is weaving and weaving thy winding-sheet,
My beautiful love with the dreaming eyes;
Her red tears fall and shall snare thy feet,

My passionate bird with the soft milk cries.
Her arm round thy musk-rose body she slips,
On thy face the grey sorrow of age is thrown;
Her leering mouth brushes the dew from thy lips:
My own! My own!
My beautiful love with the dreaming eyes.

PATRICK GALVIN

With My Little Red Knife

With my little red knife
I met my love
With my little red knife
I courted
And she stole me to her deep down bed
Her hair spread out a furnace red
But never a tender word was said
About my little red knife

With my little red knife
I held her down
With my little red knife
I kissed her
And there in the sleep of her two blue eyes
I kissed and kissed a thousand lies
And opened wide her golden thighs
To please my little red knife

With my little red knife
I made her weep
With my little red knife
I loved her
The wine was heavy in her mouth

The morning air stood up to shout
But there wasn't a living soul about
To see my little red knife

With my little red knife
I raised her up
With my little red knife
I ripped her
And there in the gloom and rolling night
I cut her throat by candlelight
And hurried home to my waiting wife
Who damned my little red knife.

J. M. SYNGE

With One Long Kiss

With one long kiss
Were you nearby
You'd break the dismal cloud that is
On all my sky

With one long kiss
If you were near
You'd sweeten days I take amiss
When lonely here.

With one long kiss
You'd make for me
A golden paradise of this
Day's beggary

THOMAS KINSELLA

Woe to Him Who Slanders Women

From the Irish of Gerald Fitzgerald, 4th Earl of Desmond

Woe to him who slanders women.
Scorning them is no right thing.
All the blame they've ever had
is undeserved, of that I'm sure.

Sweet their speech and neat their voices.
They are a sort I dearly love.
Woe to the reckless who revile them.
Woe to him who slanders women.

Treason, killing, they won't commit
nor any loathsome, hateful thing.
Church or bell they won't profane.
Woe to him who slanders women.

But for women we would have,
for certain, neither kings nor prelates,
prophets mighty, free from fault.
Woe to him who slanders women.

They are the victims of their hearts.
They love a sound and slender man
—not soon do they dislike the same.
Woe to him who slanders women.

Ancient persons, stout and grey,
they will not choose for company,
but choose a juicy branch, though poor.
Woe to him who slanders women!

PAUL MULDOON

Something of a Departure

Would you be an angel
And let me rest,
This one last time,
Near that plum-colored beauty spot
Just below your right buttock?

Elizabeth, Elizabeth,
Had words not escaped us both
I would have liked to hear you sing
'Farewell to Tarwathie'
Or 'Ramble Away.'

Your thigh, your breast,
Your wrist, the ankle
That might yet sprout a wing—
You're altogether as slim
As the chance of our meeting again.

So put your best foot forward
And steady, steady on.
Show me the plum-colored beauty spot
Just below your right buttock,
And take it like a man.

WILLIAM LARMINIE

Consolation

Yes, let us speak; with lips confirming
The inner pledge that your eyes reveal;—
Bright eyes that death shall dim for ever,
And lips that silence soon shall seal.

Yes, let us make our claim recorded
Against the powers of earth and sky,
And that cold boon their laws award us—
Just once to live, and once to die.

Thou say'st that fate is frosty nothing,
But love the flame of souls that are:—
'Two spirits approach and at their touching
Behold an everlasting star!'

High thoughts, O love; well!—let us speak them!
Yet bravely face at least this fate,—
To know the dreams of us that dream them
On blind unknowing things await.

If years from winters' chill recover,
If fields are green and rivers run;

If thou and I behold each other,
Hangs it not all on yonder sun?

So, while that mighty lord is gracious
With prodigal beam to flood the skies,
Let us be glad that he can spare us
The light to kindle lovers' eyes.

And die assured should life's new wonder,
In any world our slumbers break,
These the first words that each will utter,
'Beloved, art thou too awake?'

EITHNE CAVANAGH

Return to Avondale

You, my love, encourage me
to roll down Parnell's sloping sward.
I want to spin forever
close to pungent earth
reclaiming childhood pleasure,
trees centrifuged against the sky.

We turn another year, my love,
Your 'Bravo' assaults
the pounding inner ear
as I reel, unfocussed, dizzy,
towards snap of tourist lens.
I already see the caption
'Mature Irishwoman at Play'.

PAUL DURCAN

She Mends an Ancient Wireless

You never claimed to be someone special;
Sometimes you said you had no special talent;
Yet I have seen you rear two dancing daughters
With care and patience and love unstinted;
Reading or telling stories, knitting gansies
And all the while holding down a job
In the teeming city, morning until dusk.
And in the house whenever anything went wrong
You were the one who fixed it without fuss;
The electricity switch which was neither on nor off,
The TV aerial forever falling out;
And now as I watch you mend an ancient wireless
From my tiny perch I cry once more your praises
And call out your name across the great divide—Nessa

Padraic Fallon

Parfum Exotique

Your body this humid afternoon is another
Climate, your breast a tropic I take over,
Geography a sultry odour, aromas of you when
I lie headlong on a new-found equator

An island listing to the Trades drops fruit
Down the tilted south; big mincing buckes
Laze on the skyline and your blood-sisters flit
By, outstaring me with insolent good looks.

Here are the regions native to your flesh
A drugged seahaven, ships at the wall
With cockbilled yards, broken from seas too tall

And the green tamarinds, the odour of—and the mess
Mix in the salt world drifting off your skin
With the sailaway chanties of the deepwater men.

Medbh McGuckian

On Not Being Your Lover

Your eyes were ever brown, the colour
Of time's submissiveness. Love nerves
Or a heart, beat in their world of
Privilege, I had not yet kissed you
On the mouth.

But I would not say, in my un-freedom
I had weakly drifted there, like the
Bone-deep blue that visits and decants
The eyes of our children:

How warm and well-spaced their dreams
You can tell from the sleep-late mornings
Taken out of my face! Each lighted
Window shows me cardiganed, more desolate
Than the garden, and more hallowed
Than the hinge of the brass-studded
Door that we close, and no one opens,
That we open and no one closes.

In a far-flung, too young part,
I remembered all your slender but
Persistent volume said, friendly, complex
As the needs of your new and childfree girl.

Edward Dowden

Old Letters

Your letters flinging their good seed—
Wit, counsel, wisdom, thought—
Words that could shape my dream, my deed,
I miss them, do I not?

Yes, but how words dissect, divide
Our truths; their swiftest play
Hastens too slowly, strikes too wide,
Falters or falls away.

And now our meanings, whole and sole,
From sense to spirit outleap;
Truth now with joy is integral,
Deep answers unto deep.

So when speech comes to claim its share,
We feel, all words beneath,
Tremblings of heart oracular,
Accords of life and death.

PERMISSIONS ACKNOWLEDGEMENTS

We are grateful to the copyright holders for permission to include the poems listed below.

AE (George Russell), 'Forgiveness', reprinted by permission of Colin Smythe Ltd.

AE (George Russell), 'Illusion', reprinted by permission of Colin Smythe Ltd.

Alfred Allen, 'Love and the Years', reprinted by permission of the author.

Fergus Allen, 'Way Back Then', 'A Time for Blushing', reprinted by permission of Faber & Faber Ltd.

Samuel Beckett, 'Cascando', reprinted by permission of The Samuel Beckett Estate and The Calder Educational Trust.

Eavan Boland, 'Ready for Flight' and 'The Other Woman' from *Collected Poems*, published by Carcanet Press, reprinted by permission of the publisher.

Dermot Bolger, 'From the Lament for Arthur Cleary', from *Taking My Letters Back*, New & Selected Poems of Dermot Bolger (New Island Books). Reprinted by permission of the author.

Joseph Campbell, 'Sighle of the Lovespot', reprinted by permission of Simon Campbell.

Siobhán Campbell, 'The Chairmaker', reprinted by permission of the publisher.

Eithne Cavanagh, 'Return to Avondale', reprinted by permission of the author.

Austin Clarke, 'Flower-Quiet in the Rush-Strewn Shieling', 'Gracey Nugent', 'The Envy of Poor Lovers', 'The Planter's Daughter', reprinted by permission of R. Dardis Clarke, 21 Pleasants Street, Dublin 8.

Padraic Colum, 'She Moved Through the Fair', reprinted by permission of Maire Colum O'Sullivan.

Maurice James Craig, 'Love Poem', reprinted by permission of the author.

Anthony Cronin, 'Surprise', reprinted by permission of the author.

Denis Devlin, 'Wishes for Her', reprinted by permission of the publisher.

Myles Dillon, 'Farewell to Last Night', reprinted by permission of John Dillon.

Maura Dooley, 'At *Les Deux Magots*', from *Explaining Magnetism*, Bloodaxe Books, 1991, reprinted by permission of the publisher.

Theo Dorgan, 'Death Will Come', 'Up All Night' (translated from the 18th century Irish), reprinted by permission of the author.

Paul Durcan, 'Martha's Wall', 'Nessa', 'Sally', 'She Mends an Ancient Wireless', 'The Difficulty That Is Marriage', reprinted by permission of the author.

Padraic Fallon, 'Mary Hynes', 'Parfum Exotique', 'The Poems of Love', from *Collected Poems*, published by Carcanet Press, reprinted by permission of the publisher.

Fanning Micheál, 'Consolation', from *Verbum et Verbum*, Salmon Publishing Ltd, 1997, reprinted by permission of the publisher.

Gabriel Fitzmaurice, 'In the Midst of Possibility', 'Entanglement' (translated from the Irish of Caitlin Maude), reprinted by permission of the author.

Gabriel Fitzmaurice, 'The Search', a translation from the Irish of Gabriel Rosenstock, reprinted by permission of the translator.

Patrick Galvin, 'My Little Red Knife', reprinted by permission of the author.

Oliver St John Gogarty, 'Good Luck', reprinted by permission of Colin Smythe Ltd.

Oliver St John Gogarty, 'Leda and the Swan', reprinted by permission of Colin Smythe Ltd.

Oliver St John Gogarty, 'Perfection', reprinted by permission of Colin Smythe Ltd.

Oliver St John Gogarty, 'Tell Me Now', reprinted by permission of Colin Smythe Ltd.

Lady Isabella Augusta Gregory, 'Donall Oge; Grief of a Girl's Heart', reprinted by permission of Colin Smythe Ltd.

Lady Isabella Augusta Gregory, 'The Day Draws Near', reprinted by permission of Colin Smythe Ltd.

Lady Isabella Augusta Gregory, 'The Enchanted Mistress', reprinted by permission of Colin Smythe Ltd.

Lady Isabella Augusta Gregory, 'Will You Be As Hard?', reprinted by permission of Colin Smythe Ltd.

Lady Isabella Augusta Gregory, 'What Have I Gained?', reprinted by permission of Colin Smythe Ltd.

James Harpur, 'The Young Man of Galway's Lament', from *The Monk's Dream*, Anvil Press Poetry, 1996, reprinted by permission of the publisher.

Michael Hartnett, 'Quicksand', 'I Cannot Lie Here Anymore', translated from the Irish of Nuala Ní Dhomhnaill, from *Selected Poems* (1993), Raven Arts Press, reprinted by kind permission of The Gallery Press.

Seamus Heaney, 'Bedside Reading', 'The Otter', reprinted by permission of Faber & Faber Ltd.

John Hewitt, 'From *Sonnets for Roberta*', reprinted by permission of The Blackstaff Press.

Pearse Hutchinson, 'Into Their True Gentleness', from *Watching the Morning Grow*, 1972, reprinted by kind permission of the author and The Gallery Press.

Douglas Hyde, 'I Shall Not Die for Thee', 'My Grief on the Sea', 'Ringleted Youth of My Love', 'Will You Be As Hard?', reprinted by permission of Douglas Sealy.

Valentin Iremonger, 'Hector', reprinted by permission of Avril Iremonger.

James Joyce, 'XXXVI', from *James Joyce: Poems and Shorter Writings*, Faber & Faber, London (1991). The poem is reproduced with the permission of the Estate of James Joyce; © copyright, Estate of James Joyce.

Patrick Kavanagh, 'Bluebells for Love', by kind permission of the Trustees of the Estate of Patrick Kavanagh, c/o Peter Fallon, Literary Agent, Loughcrew, Oldcastle, Co. Meath, Ireland.

Maeve Kelly, 'Half Century', from *Resolution*, Blackstaff Press, 1986, reprinted by permission of the author.

Brendan Kennelly, 'A Love-Song', 'Reconciliation', from *Love of Ireland poems from the Irish by Brendan Kennelly*, Mercier Press, Cork, Ireland, reprinted by permission of the publisher.

Brendan Kennelly, 'A Restoration', 'Love-Cry', 'The Scarf', 'Wings', from *A Time for Voices: Selected Poems 1960–1990*, Bloodaxe Books, reprinted by permission of the publisher.

Thomas Kinsella, 'Lay Your Weapons Down, Young Lady' (translated from the Irish of Piaras Feiritear), 'Tête à Tête', 'Woe to Him Who Slanders Women' (translated from the Irish of Gerald FitzGerald, 4th Earl of Desmond), 'Yourself and Myself', reprinted by permission of the author.

Michael Longley, 'A Touch', 'In Mayo', 'The Linen Industry', reprinted by permission of the author.

Máire Mhac an Tsaoi, 'Finit', 'Jack', 'No Second Deirdre', reprinted by permission of the author.

Thomas MacGreevy, 'Dechtire', reprinted by permission of Margaret Farrington and Elizabeth Ryan.

Patrick MacDonogh, 'She Walked Unaware', reprinted by permission of Caroline MacDonogh.

Roy McFadden, 'Epithalamium', from *Flowers for a Lady* (1926), Routledge, reprinted by permission of the publisher.

Mebdh McGuckian, 'On Not Being Your Lover', from *Venus and The Rain*, Revised Edition (1994), and *Selected Poems* (1997), reprinted by kind permission of the author and The Gallery Press.

Brian MacGuigan, 'Contentment', reprinted by permission of the author.

Louis MacNeice, 'Cradle Song for Eleanor', 'The Introduction', from *Collected Poems*, Faber & Faber, reprinted by permission of David Higham Associates.

Derek Mahon, 'The Old Snaps', from *Collected Poems* 1999, reprinted by kind permission of the author and The Gallery Press.

Hugh Maxton, 'Dialectique', 'Failing to Translate', reprinted by permission of the author.

John Montague, 'Refrain' (from the poem 'Tearing 98'), from *Collected Poems*, 1995, reprinted by kind permission of the author, The Gallery Press and Wake Forest University Press.

Paul Muldoon, 'Something of a Departure', reprinted by permission of Faber & Faber Ltd.

Richard Murphy, 'Moonshine', from *Collected Poems* (2000), reprinted by kind permission of the author and The Gallery Press.

Eilean Ní Chuilleanáin, From 'The Rose Geranium IV', from *The Rose Geranium* (1981), reprinted by kind permission of the author and Gallery Press.

Nuala Ní Dhomhnaill, 'I Cannot Lie Here Anymore', 'Shannon Estuary', 'Quicksand', reprinted by permission of the author.

Frank O'Connor, 'A Learned Mistress', 'Exile', 'The Body's Speech', 'The Unmarried Clergy' (translated from the Irish of Brian Merriman), 'To The Lady with a Book' reprinted by permission of Mrs Harriet O'Donovan Sheehy.

Ulick O'Connor, 'Oscar Wilde', reprinted by permission of the author.

Desmond O'Grady, 'In the Greenwood', 'The Love War', reprinted by permission of the author.

Micheal O'Siadhail, 'Welcome', from *Poems 1975–1995*, Bloodaxe Books 1999, reprinted by permission of the publisher.

W. R. Rodgers, 'The Lovers', 'The Net', from *Poems* (1986), reprinted by kind permission of the author and The Gallery Press.

Gabriel Rosenstock, 'The Search', reprinted by permission of the author.

James Stephens, 'The Coolin', reprinted by permission of the Society of Authors as the literary representative of the Estate of James Stephens.

Katherine Tynan, 'Blind Country', 'I Wonder Why', 'The Dead-Tryst', reprinted by permission of Mr Alec Hinkson.

W. B. Yeats, 'The Lover Mourns for the Loss of Love', 'The Song of Wandering Aengus', from *The Wind Among the Reeds* (1899), 'The Folly of Being Comforted', from *In the Seven Woods* (1903), 'The Cold Heaven', from *The Green Helmet* (1912), reprinted by permission of A.P. Watt Ltd, on behalf of Michael B. Yeats.

Augustus Young, 'She's My Love', reprinted by permission of the author.

Jeremy Young, 'True Love', reprinted by permission of the author.

Every effort has been made to trace and contact copyright holders. If there are any inadvertent omissions in the acknowledgements we apologise to those concerned.

INDEX